A Love DEEPER THAN THE OCEAN

*You Are Not Alone On Your Journey To Heal
After Childhood Abuse: A True Story of Love, Betrayal,
Hate and Divine Forgiveness*

MARIE CASTELLANO

BALBOA.PRESS
A DIVISION OF HAY HOUSE

Balboa Press books may be ordered through booksellers or by contacting:

Balboa Press
A Division of Hay House
1663 Liberty Drive
Bloomington, IN 47403
www.balboapress.com
844-682-1282

Print information available on the last page.

ISBN: 979-8-7652-4654-2 (sc)
ISBN: 979-8-7652-4653-5 (e)

Library of Congress Control Number: 2023920464

Balboa Press rev. date: 11/15/2023

DEAR READER

I was an expert on believing I'm not good enough. For at least the first 30 decades of my life, I believed that I was a "stupid, piece of shit, asshole." Those are the words my father would drill into my head almost daily when he was angry about something; and he was often angry. He would get in moods that were both frightening and violent. I was constantly being reminded that I would never amount to anything good.

For a significant portion of my life, I carried around the belief that I simply did not measure up to those who had more money than I did. They certainly had better educations. They were doctors, lawyers, teachers, psychologists and psychiatrists, even writers. In my eyes, they stood head and shoulders above me, possessing better educations, illustrious professions, and esteemed degrees in English and the Literary Arts, as well as History, Science and Mathematics. These were all people who occupied a higher rung on the social ladder than I did. They were undoubtedly more intelligent, more accomplished, and more important than I could ever hope to be. This mindset weighed heavily on me, causing me to constantly question my own worth and abilities. I felt as though I was living in a world that had been designed for and by people who were simply better than I was.

However, as time passed and I gained more life experience, I began to realize the fallacy of my thinking. I came to understand that intelligence and education were not the sole determinants of a person's value or worth. I learned that every individual has their unique strengths, talents, and qualities that contribute to the fabric of society. Life is not a competition, nor is it a race to see who can accumulate the most wealth or accolades. Rather, it is about finding one's purpose and fulfilling it to the best of one's abilities. While some may choose to pursue prestigious professions or pursue higher education, others may find fulfillment in less conventional paths. The key is to recognize and appreciate the diversity of human experience and to celebrate the unique contributions that each individual brings to the table of Life.

Yet, all this being said, I still continued to believe that all of them were better and more important people than I could ever hope to be. They were far smarter and far superior to me. This is what happens when someone continually tells us, or even beats into us, that we are not good enough. I say: To Hell With That!

I always justified my insecurities with such words as, "I have a PhD from the school of hard knocks." And, while yes, that is true. If the School of Hard Knocks acknowledged my decades worth of pain and suffering, the decades in which I pinched, crawled and struggled to overcome the almost unsurvivable obstacles I received in my life, I would definitely be a star-student and take home my well deserved *School of Hard Knocks Diploma*, and I would do so with Honors.

Some things, some very important Life Lessons on this Earth School, cannot be learned in books. University professors cannot teach you what you must ultimately learn for yourself. They can only speak about the possibility, and the probability; they can speculate and guess. Resilience is a trait that is developed from within a person. You cannot gain Resilience from a book. That includes this book, as well. You must do the work necessary, because nobody can do it for you.

The role of university professors in the education process is undoubtedly crucial, but it is critical to recognize that they cannot provide you with all the knowledge that you must acquire. There exist certain skills, such as resilience, that are developed from within an individual and cannot be taught solely through conventional academic means. Although professors and therapists can provide theoretical frameworks and offer guidance, it is ultimately up to the childhood abuse and/or domestic abuse *victim* to develop the necessary determination and perseverance that resilience requires. While the concept of resilience can be explored through various readings and scholarly discussions, it is only through personal experiences and trials that one can truly develop this quality.

As you read this book it will become very clear to you that I have been there. I know far too well what it means to suffer at the hands of another. I know what it's like to love someone, and look up to them with the eyes of an innocent child. Only to have them take advantage of that innocence for their own sick and perverted cravings. I know what it means to truly suffer. Oftentimes, it so happens that once we have learned what it feels like to be mistreated and abused, we subconsciously believe this is all we are worthy of having in life, and we can attract more of the same.

I understand your pain, and I know how difficult and confusing it is to make any sense out of such a senseless thing. This journey you are on is not an easy one, not at all. Surviving child abuse is, in my humble opinion, one of the most heartbreaking, horrific and painful experiences a human being can experience. We were only children, for God's Sake.

I know that you have within you everything you need to not only survive, but to thrive, because it all happened for you. As hard as I'm sure this is for you to hear right now. Read on. You are going to discover something about yourself in these pages that you can put into action right here and right now.

The stories and the steps you read in each chapter are designed to start with where you are on your journey now. Each chapter builds upon what you learned about yourself in the previous chapter. It continues to teach you step-by-step with non-judgment about yourself and whatever happened in your past. It offers you a sacred space for doing the work.

You must do the work, if you want positive results. I offer you my true story as a tool that can help to touch your heart and ignite your Soul. Doing the lessons, as I lay them out for you, will stack your outer strengths, your attributes, your inner strengths, your courage; and your purpose can become clear. Your Self-Worth can be raised and your Higher Self can guide you as you learn how to Take Your Own Unique Power Back! It is, afterall, your power and yours alone. Nobody, not a parent, a step-parent, a grandparent, an uncle or aunt; not a teacher, or priest or a preacher can touch or harm your Higher Self.

They may have broken your bones, and fed you lies. They may have forced you to keep dirty, dark little secrets and stolen your innocence, but they have no real power to take your True and Authentic Self from You. This part of you is perfect. It is Divine.

You become able to see, to feel and you begin to Know

The Truth of who you really are as you read this book from beginning to end. Do the work as I lay it out for you and the Truth of Who You Truly Are Can Set You Free!

Sending You All Strength, Courage and Love, as You Make The Journey Back To You,

Marie Castellano, XOXOXO

HOW TO READ THIS BOOK

Each chapter is set up to help you get clear on what's blocking you and your ability to Take Your Own Personal Power Back. Most of the chapters will have a corresponding writing lesson for you. The last 3 chapters are writing or speaking lessons for you, in and of themselves.

I highly suggest that you Create a Special Space to complete each lesson plan. Give yourself some much needed privacy when doing each lesson. Treat this book and the work you do for yourself as if it were your very own personal diary. This is Your Life we are talking about! A day without anger, a night without triggers, and a week with no anxiety attacks, is definitely doable. I believe in you. You got this!

If you burn incense, burn it in this sacred space of yours. Maybe you'll want to have a few candles in your sacred space. Keep the energy of this place personal, for you, and you alone, to work in. This is not a place for others to go snooping around, so please keep true to your personal boundaries and the sacred space where you choose to do this most important work. This is very important work you are doing. It may be best for some of you to not talk to others in your home about what you are doing, or at the very least, tell them that you need some alone time to read, to be with yourself, to journal, pray and meditate. Perhaps suggest to them that you are working on yourself, which can, undoubtedly, allow you to feel better and be happy. This will help you to Love better. As you love yourself, you find that you are able to give more love, understanding and hold gratitude within for others.

Creating a sacred space for oneself can be a deeply personal and spiritual experience. If you choose to incorporate incense, sage or essential oils into this space, it is important to ensure that it is only burned within this designated area. The scent of incense can be powerful and transformative, and when burned within your sacred space, it can help to create a sense of peace and tranquility. In addition to incense, consider adding other elements to your sacred space. A vase filled with beautiful flowers can bring a natural and vibrant energy to the space. Candles are another popular addition, adding a warm and comforting glow. It is crucial to remember that this space should remain personal and private.

Only you should have access to this sanctuary, and others should not be permitted to enter without your express permission. This ensures that the energy of the space remains focused and undisturbed, allowing you to fully engage in your spiritual practices without distraction. Overall, creating a sacred space can be a powerful tool for self-care and spiritual growth, and should be approached with intention and care.

If you have any special prayers you love, say them before you start reading and then do the work that this book requires. What you are doing is setting the Energy; the stage if you will. You are calling forth Your Intentions for Love, Courage, Strength, Forgiveness and Your Own Inner Peace to all join together as One to support you, as you do this most important work on yourself, for yourself.

CONTENTS

Chapter 1

ONCE UPON A TIME
IN LOS ANGELES

*H*AVE YOU EVER FELT AFRAID that you can't reveal your whole self, i.e., your true story, to others because you fear that they will judge you, they might not believe you or maybe won't love you anymore? If your answer is yes, I understand how you feel. I have been there. I felt the same fears, too.

Hello, My name is Marie, and I wrote this beautiful book to show you how you can change the negative patterns you have been living, as a result of your being abused, and how you can learn how to be authentic and genuine; to show you how you can reconnect to your Purpose, which is ultimately, your Higher Self. As the proverb goes, "Every cloud has a silver lining." I believe this applies to all of us. Let me share my insights and my true life story with you.

The story you are about to read is true. Some of the names have been changed or not used at all. To the very best of my recollection, these events happened exactly as I say they did. This is, after all, My True Story.

Imagine, if you will, it's the 1960's. I don't really remember much of my childhood before I was 4 years old, so this is the best place for me to set the scene for you. Please, grab some tissues, some water and welcome to my story:

I was born under the sign of Taurus, for those of you who love all things, Astrology. I was the 5th, and final, child for my parents. My place in the pecking order in my family was last. Coming in last has its pros and its cons.

1960 something gave us Meet the Beatles! Yeah, yeah, yeah!!! Yeaaaah!!! I believed that I was supposed to grow up and marry the *cute* Beatle, Paul McCartney, but apparently the Royal Mail was slow and Paul, er ah, Sir Paul, sadly, still has not received the message.

As a little girl, I had it all planned out. I used to play with my Barbie dolls and Ken was renamed, Paul, of course, as in Paul McCartney. Barbie was renamed, Pauline. Paul and Pauline were married, and they lived happily ever after, with their children, Paul Jr., Penelope, and Penny, who were twin girls. I was raised as a Catholic, and in the 60's in Los Angeles, CA, specifically the San Fernando Valley, most of my neighbors were also Catholic, or Jewish, and many of them had rather large families.

Over the years, Paul and Pauline McCartney grew their beautiful and very happy family with two more perfect children, Peter, and Polly. I'm not sure why I named all of my Barbie dolls with the letter P. Somehow, in my most innocent mind, it made them all extra-special close as a loving family and although they were a very make-believe family, I lived vicariously through their daily lives. Their adventures were my adventures, and their quite obvious strong family bond and unconditional love for each other became my own.

I loved dogs and horses back then; I still do. We had a

family dog, her name was Terry. I loved her to her dying day and long after that. I still miss her. I love animals, especially dogs, horses, and ponies. Terry was a Collie mix, probably a Terrier/Collie mix. She was brown and white. She was a medium-sized dog. She loved me and I loved her. My relationship with this dog becomes very important later on in my story. Remember, I'm a Taurus, so my loyalties run strong and I'm Tenacious, with a capital T.

The Barbie dolls, aka, the Paul McCartney Family, also loved dogs, horses and ponies. Chip chip Cheerio! Paul had his very large Morgan horse, Pauline had her beautiful Golden Palomino, Paul Jr., had his very own Thoroughbred Horse, and the Twins, Penelope and Penny each had their own Welsh Ponies. Peter and Polly, both had Shetland Ponies. They spent days on end together as one big, happy family in their horse arena during horseback riding lessons. They had such fun as the horses and ponies trotted, galloped and cantered all around their beautiful, lush, green lands. Often, they jumped competitively in Steeplechase events in the horse arena. They worked hard and practiced both day and night. The children were very dedicated and loved their horses. They entered in all sorts of jumping contests, and racing competitions. The children's rooms boasted displays of beautiful trophies and colorful ribbons! Life was excellent in the McCartney household. But, alas, it was just my imagination, running away with me.

Dogs, i.e., fake, plastic ones, were everywhere. Big dogs and little dogs, dogs that would run alongside the horses as they galloped and dogs that lazily laid down in the cool, tall, lush green grass, soaking up the English countryside, aka, the midday Southern California sun. The McCartney family each washed their horses after riding, put away all their horse tack, and gave their horses and ponies the best of care as they treated their horses with megadoses of TLC.

I had a rather large collection of horses and ponies (think statues) and I would pretend the McCartney's were riding on them. Some of the horses and ponies came with exquisite floral tooling saddles; some with suede seats. They had an entire host of quality, fancy-stitched bridles, and a wide variety of colorful horse blankets. One blanket, in particular, was a favorite of mine to put on Pauline's gorgeous Palomino. It was a deep purple and against the golden hue of her horse, it was absolutely gorgeous! I could sit in my room for hours playing with my Barbie dolls. My friends and I would meet in the front yard of one of our houses, we would carefully lay out blankets, and we would create a huge Barbie Land. We would play with those dolls from before lunch to the time our mothers would call each one of us in for supper. Good times! Really, really good times.

Growing up in my family was not easy. While I had fun at times, it was never consistently a loving, easygoing, far from dramatic and far from dysfunctional atmosphere, to say the least. I was born just in time to be old enough to appreciate The Beatles when they first hit the American Rock 'n' Roll scene in 1964, but too young to attend their live concerts at the Hollywood Bowl with my older brother and sisters. Years later, I did get to see Paul McCartney and Wings in concert at the Sports Arena in Los Angeles, CA. I have always been a Paul McCartney is the cute Beatle kinda girl. Music was, and still is, my safe haven, my escape, my Rock 'n' Roll fantasy. Music soothed my savage beast, inspired my soul and gave me strength and courage when I needed it most.

I was born in Los Angeles, CA. Precisely, Hollywood, in Kaiser Hospital on Sunset Blvd. I always thought that fact alone should buy me a ticket as a Hollywood movie star. I love acting, and yes, I am actually very good at it. My talents, my gifts, my purpose, all took a back-burner approach, or so

I thought, because of life happening to me. I have certainly experienced my fair share of Life's proverbial ups and downs. The thoughts and beliefs I held about myself, back then, were a roller coaster ride of "I'm not good enough, and I'm never going to amount to anything good." Can you relate to this? Yes, I thought so, most of us do.

Being born the fifth child to parents of five children had its ups and downs. The ups were fantastic and the downs were about as low as a human being could get. Let's start at the beginning. Let's start with the ups! Having been born #5 is tantamount to being the 5th Beatle. It just doesn't quite work.

I had two older sisters and two older brothers. My oldest sister was more like a mother to me. She was 12 years older than me. Next in line is my oldest brother who is 10 years older, and then, another sister, who thinks she is only 5 years older than me, but, alas, she is 7 years older. Finally, there's another brother, who is 5 years older than I am. Knowing the age differences between me and my siblings may not seem that necessary for you to know now, but it will make more sense to you as you continue to read.

Our household, it seemed to me growing up, was quite normal. We lived in a somewhat, upper middle-class home, in a somewhat, upper middle-class neighborhood. As a young child, I played baseball on our neighborhood streets with my friends, and during the summer months, we would stay out playing, until just after dark, around 9:00 PM. As I mentioned before, I had my Barbie collection of dolls, and my friends and I would bring all of our Barbie sets, clothes, shoes, all of our Barbie suitcases filled with mirrors, lipsticks, pretend dogs, pretend horses, and cars, campers, etc., to ensure we would have plenty of Barbie Land fun for hours upon hours in our front yards.

When we were not playing baseball or Barbies, we

would play Duck Duck Goose, Mother, May I? and Hide 'n' Seek. We rigorously fought in pretend wars as Indians vs Cowboys, and when the pretend wars were over we played on the swingset in the backyard of one of our neighbors.

We sang all of our favorite songs, loud, very, very loud! Sometimes we had campouts, aka, sleep-overs, in the playhouse in one of my friend's backyard. There were days when we all got along and there were also days when we disagreed on issues that we thought were important. When we disagreed, we fought. Sometimes we threw our Barbies and other times we tried physical fighting. Then we would go home and get in trouble with our parents for fighting. All in all, it seemed like a perfectly normal childhood to me.

I was a little girl, tiny, innocent and so very naive. Completely unaware of the ugliness that can overtake the human mind. I was both ignorant and blind to the evilness that smothered the world, and all that was lurking in hiding places within the perceived safety of my home. I trusted in my mother and father, and in my two older brothers and two older sisters, that I was completely safe and living a totally normal life.

Everything in my 5-year-old mind seemed perfectly normal. We went on family adventures every year during summer vacation from school, and although there was an age gap between us, we had good times playing games, watching tv, going to movies, we spent countless hours at the beach with many summer trips to Disneyland, Knotts Berry Farm and SeaWorld. We ventured out in the CA forests on camping trips every so many years. Most of my friends in the neighborhood were doing the same things, so I grew up thinking that I had a good, very happy, good-good life. Sure my dad would get mad at one of my siblings from time to time, and have arguments with mom, but that was all normal, right? I saw many of my friends and family members have arguments, too. Ok, we weren't the Cleavers, or the Cunningham's but we were normal.

Like most young girls my age, I always wanted a pony. Most of my friends did not receive one. I on the other hand, well, I was persistent and tenacious in my just cause, so when a neighbor received a pony for his birthday, but his parents decided that he was too young for it, and said they were going to sell it – I badgered my parents to buy it for me. I tried being smart and coy. I would find a way that I could negotiate my housework, doing the dishes, doing anything that they thought was necessary, so that I could earn that pony. When someone else ended up buying "my" pony, I was devastated.

I loved dogs, ponies and horses the most, but I always had a huge love and respect for all animals. I seemed to have some sort of a Vulcan mind-meld with animals, it was as if I was some sort of a natural dog, horse, pony, bunny, duck, guinea pig and chipmunk Whisperer of sorts. I AM an Empath. My Empathic abilities are very strong, there's no doubt about that. With the exception of one of my brothers, nobody in my family, including my sons, knows what it means to be an Empath[1]. Maybe they don't know that Empath's exist?

I think my deep affection and admiration for animals developed from witnessing conflicts among my friends and within my family. Being considerably younger than my siblings, I absorbed the stress and fear that lingered during these arguments over the years. In response, my sanctuary became our backyard.

Several months later, Kathy, my best friend in elementary school, lived in a house with her father, stepmother and her

---

[1] "15 Signs You Might Be an Empath - Healthline." https://www. healthline.com/health/what-is-an-empath. Accessed 15 Aug. 2023.

younger brother; and they were all avid horseback riders. Kathy had a little pony named Teddy Bear – Teddy, for short. Teddy was a Shetland pony, with a pinto coat. He had brown and white markings with a big, round, perfectly formed, brown circle on his back side and his long, beautiful, blonde tail grew right out from the center of that brown circle. After school I would often go to Kathy's house.

We would walk together and she would teach me how to ride Teddy. She started "lunging" with him, which is where she stood in the middle of the horse arena. He had a halter on his muzzle with a thick, blue lead rope attached, and she would have him trot in circles. If she wanted him to go faster she would just make a signal with her hand or move that lead; and he would know to go faster. Kathy and her family were horse-people, they loved their horses, they respected them, and they took excellent care of them.

Kathy would give me a *leg-up*, which is horsespeak for holding your hands in a clasped fashion and making a sort of stirrup with them, so the rider can put their foot on your hands as they hold onto the saddle horn and pull themselves up and over onto their horse. She would help me get on top of Teddy's back without having reins and nothing but a little bit of his mane to hold onto. She taught me how to use my leg muscles which eventually helped me to stay on top of him without falling off. These were my first real horseback riding lessons.

I rode Teddy without a saddle, because Kathy wanted me to get used to using my legs and my balance to keep from falling off of him, instead of relying on the saddle horn and stirrups. Everyday, after school, for the most part, that's what we did. She taught me how to ride in the arena, for hours upon hours, almost every day after school and then again on weekends when she didn't have family outings to attend. Kathy taught me how to ride Teddy and I was hooked. I loved every single minute of my training, and I loved Teddy, he was such a sweet, playful little pony. I still miss him dearly.

Then it happened! It was one very special day! On this most fabulous of days, Kathy told me that her father explained to her that she was getting too big for Teddy and that she must now start riding their much larger horses and sadly, that they were going to have to put Teddy up for sale. She wanted to know if maybe my parents would like to buy him for me. I thought that was the greatest news ever and immediately, after my riding lesson, I rushed home to talk my mom into letting me get Teddy for my own! Think: Marie needs a Shetland Pony version of Ralphie Parker's schemes to get his parents to tell Santa Claus he needs a Red Ryder Range carbine-action, 200-Shot BB Air Rifle, with a compass in the stock, and "this thing which tells time."

My mother worked tirelessly. She was constantly working in our home, cooking three plus meals a day, doing laundry, cleaning, dusting, and she also worked a job away from home. When I was old enough to help her with the household chores, I did. I guess this is where I learned how to enjoy doing housework. It must be some form of working meditation for me.

She started going to work away from home once I was old enough to go to school. Before that, she stayed home with me because my older brothers and sisters were either in school or had already graduated from high school and were living in their own places and had moved out of our home.

Teddy was for sale at the whopping price of $75 US dollars, and by today's standards that sounds like not much money at all, and it really wasn't. He was a young Pony, and he was in excellent health. Kathy and her parents kept excellent records on all of their horses. Every horse, including

Teddy, received regular vaccinations, shoeing, worming, regular vet checks, bathing supplies and of course, lots of feed and grain; with the occasional sugar cube to make the medicine go down. I learned it all, I watched it all, I loved it all.

This time I was not going to take no for an answer. My mother knew I had put in the work and she knew I could ride. She knew I learned, quite well, how to take care of a pony. She talked with Kathy's father and her stepmother, and she had their assurance that purchasing Teddy for $75 was a bargain. My mother said yes and I was beyond happy, I was the happiest little girl in the world! I had my pony! I absolutely adored Teddy just like I absolutely adored our family dog who I practically grew up with; Terry, Teddy, and I were inseparable.

Every waking moment I had when not going to school, not going to church on Sunday, not cleaning up after dinner, washing the kitchen sink, doing dishes, feeding our dog, taking my dog out for walks; every single opportunity I had to be with that sweet pony was all I cared about. I spent day after day after day riding him, learning how to jump with him, learning about his tack, learning as much as I could about Horsemanship, or in Teddy's case, Ponyship. Sometimes Kathy and her family would trailer the horses and go to horse shows. I'm not exactly sure where they were. It seemed like we traveled a long distance, but when we finally arrived at our destination, it was fantastic, because there were horses and ponies everywhere.

With eyes wide opened, I watched all the Cowboys and Cowgirls showing and riding their horses. Kathy would always compete at these events. She Barrel Raced, and eventually she taught me how to Barrel Race. She was a very accomplished horseback rider. She won many colorful ribbons and trophies. Her entire family were all excellent riders. Kathy was my very best friend and while I had friends who lived in my neighborhood and other friends from school, she was my very best friend. We shared a huge love for Teddy Bear and for all of her other horses. I think this is when I was the happiest in my childhood, my memories of Kathy, her brother, her father and her step-mother, were some of the best times, the fondest memories I ever had as a young girl and certainly some of the most meaningful.

I already had responsibilities with making sure I fed our dog her breakfast daily.

I made sure I cleaned her food and water bowls and also fed her dinner. I had responsibilities to clean, help with the dishes after dinner and wash and clean the kitchen sink with Ajax. My father liked our kitchen sink, very clean and white. Kathy taught me about horsemanship. She taught me how to put a bridle on Teddy. I learned how to saddle him. I learned how to clean his tiny, little hooves with a hoof pick. I learned how to be safe when walking in the horse stalls and also in the riding arena, and not get hurt and to make sure I never hurt him. Not bad in terms of having responsibilities for a little girl.

My friends and I used to get on our ponies and ride a mile or two to our friendly neighborhood drugstore, because the store had an ice cream bar. We each carefully tied up our pony reins onto the bicycle rack, and a few of us would stay with them. A few of us went in and bought the ice cream. I always ordered a one-scoop Vanilla ice cream for Teddy. He loved to eat his ice cream cone. The ponies would definitely leave a mess on the pavement out in front of the store, but nobody ever complained. Someone would wash away the ice cream stains. I miss those days. These were the days when children could just be children. They could go far from home and still be safe. They could play outside and really not be worried about someone hurting them.

We were told by our parents to stay together, and don't talk to strangers and all those parental warnings we received. We just had fun. Nothing bad ever happened to us. One day on our way back from a ride, I heard a lot of screaming and lots of noise. I looked down the street and I saw a little black pony, running up the street, full speed ahead, straight towards me. I thought to myself, "It's Midnight!" "What is Midnight doing out loose, running down the street?" I could see my friend and her family frantically running behind Midnight. She ran into a field of mostly just dirt and a few trees. I got off of Teddy, and tied him securely to a large tree. Midnight was running quite fast in circles around the dirt path. I walked over to the side of one of the larger trees. I was determined to catch her, because she did have her bridle on, and if I could just grab onto one of those reins, I knew I would be able to catch her.

Midnight had other plans. Everyone was trying their very best to catch her. As she turned the circle and made her way toward me, I made a slow, but deliberate step forward to grab onto one of the reins. I didn't stand a chance. She saw me and I will never forget the look in her eye as she kicked. She kicked me as I grabbed the reins, and although I was able to get her to stop, She kicked me good and hard in my upper inside left thigh! Ouch! She kicked hard for such a tiny Shetland Pony. It started swelling up and it hurt. Someone ran to my house and told my parents. Lesson learned.

Note To Self: Never, ever try to sneak up on a loose, running Shetland Pony. They are a lot stronger and faster than you are. I remember, still to this day, what the ER Physician told my parents. He said, "It's a very good thing that it was a pony that kicked her and not a horse, and it did not have horseshoes on, if it did, it could have been much worse. Your daughter may not have been able to have children." I had Midnight's hoove imprinted on my upper inner thigh, it was raised and swollen, and it hurt like hell, just like the Hell that was lurking around the corner for me.

What Are Your Takeaways?

As I share my story with you, allow yourself to think back to all the things you did in order to survive. He, She or They are no longer able to hurt you. Write about what you did in order to survive. What decisions did you make? What did you tell yourself about why it was happening?

Take some time, preferably in your sacred space, whatever that space may be for you, and write in your journal, or on a simple notepad if you choose. Our stories were very different and our abusers were different people, the circumstances we found ourselves in were different; and even though all that is true, we are very much the same in terms of what those experiences caused us to believe about ourselves and how those experiences made us feel. Your healing can manifest for you when you work through the trauma.

Ask yourself the following questions:

1. What was your childhood like BEFORE the abuse started?
2. Make a list of the happiest childhood memories you have.
3. Who were the people you were the happiest with?
4. If you don't have any happy childhood memories, write yourself a letter about what the circumstances were that caused your unhappiness.
5. If you have absolutely no memories of anything happy because you were abused at such a young age, please write something about what you are happy about, now that you are an adult and free from the abuse.

Chapter 2
MY DAD WAS MY HERO

*S*OMETIMES MY MIND DRIFTS TO the endless possibilities when it came to buying birthday gifts, Father's Day gifts, and Christmas gifts for my beloved father. In those moments, I found myself immersed in a world of imagination, envisioning the delight on his face as he unwrapped those carefully chosen presents. Driven by an unwavering determination, I diligently saved every single penny from my precious allowance – every nickel, every dime, every quarter, and every dollar bill meticulously tucked away. This secret stash served a grand purpose: enabling me to set out on an arduous journey of over two miles to reach our neighborhood shopping center, where an array of treasures awaited my discerning eye. It was there that I endeavored to discover a truly extraordinary gift that would bear testament to the love and admiration I held for my dearest Daddy. I took my time and picked out beautiful ties, the most handsome pairs of socks, and often a keychain or a very soft sweater to keep him warm during the winter.

My heart brimming with excitement, I embarked on this adventure, driven by an unparalleled desire to express my deepest affection for him. My Daddy was my Hero.

I have fond memories of spending countless hours with my dad, absorbed in his captivating stories about World War II. At the tender age of 18, he made the courageous decision to enlist in the U.S. Army, driven by an unwavering determination to confront and challenge the forces of darkness. His deep conviction led him to articulate that he felt a pressing need to confront the German forces on foreign soil, to defend the principles of justice and freedom against the tyranny embodied by Adolf Hitler.

As I grew older, whispers from my mother insinuated that his motivations ran deeper than a mere sense of duty; there seemed to be an underlying desire to escape from his own troubled past and create a new future far away from the burdens that weighed heavily upon him. The complexities of my father's journey gradually became apparent to me, painting a vivid picture of a man inspired by patriotism, personal growth, and the pursuit of a brighter tomorrow.

What Are Your Takeaways?

As I continue to share my story with you, allow yourself to think back to all the things you did in order to survive. He, She or They are no longer able to hurt you. Write about what you did in order to survive. What decisions did you make? What did you tell yourself about why it was happening?

Take some time in your sacred space, whatever that may be for you, and write in your journal. Take some long, slow deep breaths, and get quiet. In your sacred space, allow your perfect answers to come up for you. Give yourself all the time you need to do this work.

Ask yourself the following questions:

1. Did you have any Heroes or Heroines in your childhood?
2. Who did you trust to take care of you?
3. Did that person, or those persons, do a good job of taking care of you?
4. If yes, why?
5. If not, why?
6. How did you feel about that as a child?
7. How do you feel about that as an Adult now?

Chapter 3

ALL GOOD THINGS MUST COME TO AN END

I HAVE BEEN, FOR THE MOST part, a happy, normal, little girl, having normal life experiences. For the most part, life was good. I was happy, carefree, high-spirited and adventurous. However, I began to realize that something was not quite right with my dad, or with my entire family, for that matter.

I did not know exactly what it was. Even though everything seemed great, and certainly normal on the outside, there was trouble brewing inside. That's Trouble with a capital T and that T stands for Trauma.

As previously mentioned, I have four older siblings. My oldest sister was 11 years older than me. Sadly, she passed away from breast cancer in December of 1999. I have never truly gotten over the pain of losing her. I loved her – in many ways she was almost like a mother to me. My older brother is 2 years younger than her, followed by my younger sister who is 2 years younger than him, and finally my youngest brother who is 2 years younger than her. I was born 5 years after my brother, making me 7 years younger than my sister and 9 years younger than my oldest brother.

The pecking order of my family is important for you to understand, because there's a huge gap in our age differences. This meant that when I was a young girl in 3rd grade, my older sister had already graduated from high school and was working. The remainder of my siblings followed in perfect chronological order. They were busy living their lives, and deciding what they wanted to be now that they were grown up, or almost grown up, and leaving the nest – or maybe they were pushed out.

I remember there were almost always, at least it seemed that way to me, arguments between my father and my mother and my brothers and sisters. He was very critical, to say the least, about their choices. Nothing ever seemed good enough for him. How could any of us believe we would ever be good enough? We didn't stand a chance. All of us had been on the receiving end of his anger at one point or another in our childhoods and we were all, including my mother at times, ingrained with the words he continually spat from his mouth, "You are a stupid, piece-of-shit, asshole!" He could burst into fits of rage at the drop of a hat. With all the time, energy and money, all the blood, sweat and tears I have spent to heal myself, and push myself to overcome my inner demons, I realized my father treated us as though we were not good enough, because he, himself, never believed he was good enough. I understand now what I could not comprehend back then when I was a child.

It wasn't all gloom and doom, however, there were other times when he was singing, laughing and acting very funny. He seemed happy. Again, my childhood was very confusing. Was all this normal? I wondered if he was stressed from working too hard. I was a young child, and while I tried my best to not pay much attention to the negative and scary arguments I could not help but hear, I was developing Asthma. The stress from watching my parents fighting, and often my dad yelling at my siblings, was taking its toll on my health, even at a very young age. Before I had reached 11, I had been stricken with double pneumonia twice.

One cold Christmas morning, Jolly Ol' Saint Nick put something, a present, for me under our Christmas Tree. I was tickled pink to receive it! It was a perfect, cuddly Teddy Bear. I loved that sweet bear. He had beautiful brown fur with some color blocking. His cute little face was brown, he had short, stubby little arms and legs; with a cute yellowish belly. His eyes were dark, and to me they were compassionate eyes. He was a wind-up Teddy Bear. He played a beautiful song in chimes. I can't remember exactly what that song was, but I certainly remember how I felt when I held onto that Bear.

Teddy Bear was my friend. He was my best friend, he was my protector. The only friend even closer to me than my Teddy bear was my beloved dog, Terry. They were both my Soul Companions, although, in reality, one of them was an inanimate object; the other one was a dog. To a young child who needed to feel safe, that little stuffed bear held her deepest fears. When I was scared and startled by the yelling coming from outside my bedroom door, I held onto that bear ever so tightly. Each time my parents had argued over something again, and as I listened as my father yelled at one of my brothers or sisters, it terrified me. It was often terrifying for me to live in that house.

It isn't that there weren't good times, there definitely were happy and fun times in that house. We had extended family over for the holidays, Grandma would come over, and it was always so lovely to see her, even if I could not speak Spanish with her. She made the best homemade

Tamales. I loved my Grandmother. There were Aunts and Uncles and Cousins whose laughter and warmhearted conversations filled our home. All us kids played outside in the yards and ran throughout the halls and rooms of that house. Thanksgiving and Christmas were always so much fun. Music filled the air, and Christmas specials were on the T.V. There was always food, lots and lots of food. Again, the word that comes up for me to sum up my childhood is *Confusing.*

During the difficult times, Teddy was always there for me to hold onto and hug. I would tell Teddy all my secrets. He was a very good listener. He never interrupted me, like some people tend to do. I would wind him up and listen to that sweet music as I attempted to pull away from the battles that lurked just outside my bedroom door.

Sometimes, I wished I could shrink down to Teddy's size and disappear. I thought to myself, maybe I could shrink down to the size of a pint-sized Alice in Wonderland, and stay that way in a hole somewhere where nobody could find me. I could wait it out until all the shouting stopped and my mother would call me to come into the kitchen and set the table for dinner.

How my family could fit into that small kitchen and then eat dinner together like it was Leave It To Beaver meets August Osage County was beyond me. I remember during one family dinner, somebody said something that pissed my father off, and with dinner spread out all over our dinner table, he smacks his hand down on the table just at the right spot to throw the table off balance and it tips over. Good thing we were not having spaghetti that night. Food was flying everywhere. In an instant, all of my mom's hard work cooking our dinner, just moments before, was now all over the place. This was not so unusual. Over the years, I came to realize that some of my friends would experience similar shouting matches in their homes as well. I wondered if this was a result of these men – these fathers – suffering from their time serving in WWII. Maybe War, and the subsequent death and destruction it breeds, created the PTSD within our neighborhood?

What Are Your Takeaways?

As I share my story with you, allow yourself to think back to all the things you did in order to survive. He, She or They are no longer able to hurt you. Write about what you did in order to survive. What decisions did you make? What did you tell yourself about why it was happening?

Maybe you want to light a candle, or burn some sage or incense. Take some time now to Breathe slowly and deeply. Settle yourself, and when you are ready go ahead and ask yourself the following questions:

1. Did you witness fits of rage in your childhood? What age were you?
2. What was the "pecking order" in your family?
3. Did you have an intuition that something was not normal?
4. What did you do, or not do in order to feel safe?
5. What Adjectives do you use to label your childhood? For example, in my particular case, my childhood was *confusing*.

Chapter 4

EVERYWHERE I LOOKED
I SAW BULLIES

As if being called a stupid, piece-of-shit, asshole by your own father, repeatedly, for decades, wasn't bad enough, all the name calling, all the family squabbles, were just the tip of the iceberg. The avalanches of abuse were just beginning along with my struggles to survive it all. Many of my neighbors judged me as being spoiled, because I had my own pony. Little did they know that the grass was not always greener at the house next door. We grow up very confused when we are living in a dysfunctional family environment. I get it. I truly understand what it means to suffer the slings and arrows of life.

Enter stage left, this is my Leon story. Leon was a boy in elementary school with me; in my 4th grade class. He was constantly picking on me. I don't know what it was about me that he hated so much. Maybe Leon actually hated himself?

The eagerly anticipated school bell rang out signifying the end of a long day at school. While on my walk home, some of the kids from school were walking on the sidewalk in front of me, and some were walking behind me. We were sort of bunched in together, because the sidewalk was not very wide. There was this boy, I'll call him Leon, who for some reason had it in for me. The adults at school would try to justify Leon's bad behavior and say it was because he liked me. Strange way of showing it, Leon. He was so full of anger and hatred. He kept trying to provoke me. I was trying to walk home. I wanted to get home to my safe place, throw my school books on my bed, grab my usual cold glass of milk and some much deserved cookies and turn on the T.V., so I could watch my favorite cartoons, and hug my dog after a long day at school.

I remember this day Leon looked particularly agitated. He started pushing me from behind. I kept my balance. I had a very small, petite frame back then. Leon kept pushing from behind and egging me on with his barrage of tough guy name calling and aggressive, perverse rude remarks. I kept trying to ignore him, but he was determined to fight. I'm talking full out fist to cuffs throwing punches. Mind you, he's a lot taller than my tiny, Pixie-self was at the time, and he was a lot stronger. He's slinging verbal arrows at me, and as hard as I tried to just ignore him, at one point, I turned around and looked him straight in the eyes, and he did not like that at all! Bam!!! He starts punching on my head like there's no tomorrow! Pow!! Bam!! He's throwing punches, closed fist after closed fist. It was all I could do to protect my head and my face from being hit by putting my arms up over my head and turning my face in the opposite direction of the onslaught of clenched fists. He eventually stops, most likely from pure exhaustion. I don't know why, but not one teacher intervened. We were off school property, but only a couple of blocks from the school. I don't really remember any of the kids trying to stop him either. It may be that they were all afraid they would be next.

I do remember this, and I will always remember it, I never allowed him to know that he hurt me. I did not cry. I did not scream. I did not react. I certainly did not give him the satisfaction of seeing me cry. I stayed calm and tough even though my face and head were swelling from the intense thrashing. I stood toe-to-toe with him, my face mere inches from his, and I asked him, "Are you done?" and "Do you feel better now?" I never allowed him to use me as his punching bag ever again, and he never did.

Sometime later, I figured out that he was getting beaten up in his own home. I found out that his dad was brutally hitting him. He wasn't just hitting him, he was pounding on him. Leon was venting his anger, his pain, and his furious frustration with his own father. It certainly did not excuse his behavior, but there was a reason for his incessant need to harm others who were innocent and a lot smaller and weaker than he was. If you struggle with anger, and you find yourself hitting your children and call it spanking, get Help NOW. Children should never be hit. They should never be beaten. This is how more violence keeps being created in the world. All you are doing is teaching your children that they are not worthy of your love and acceptance. You are only spreading hate and violence. Most likely you do this because you were also spanked, hit or beaten and mistreated as a child. Get help. Get help Now. Be a part of the solution, and never the problem. You do have a choice. You can always choose to live differently from the way you were raised. You have that choice. All you have to do is make the decision to raise your children from a place of love, respect and patience… Lots and lots of patience.

This is how patterns are developed. This is how beliefs about ourselves, our world and everyone in it are created.

This is how identities are formed. If Human Beings hold on to anything, they hold on to their Identities.

I started having boys "like" me ever since I was in elementary school. Just cute, little puppy-love stuff; with the exception of Leon who could only show a very disturbed version of "like." I can remember my so-called "boyfriends" easily, as if it were yesterday, and I was back at school, just being me, little Marie. A tiny, dark-haired, hazel-eyed girl. Like I mentioned earlier, I was skinny and very petite, however; I had the strength of a Bull. I was always running somewhere. I loved to race just about anyone, boy or girl, who would take the challenge. I won every single race I was in. I loved to run! Running for me was like being the wind. It was like being part of the wind itself. I believed I could lift up and fly away with the breeze. I used to run and wave my arms around in huge circles, thinking to myself if I just ran fast enough and circled my arms fast enough, I could lift off of the ground. There were a few times when the Santa Ana winds were blowing fiercely, in the San Fernando Valley, and I was sure that I had lift-off! Deep down, I think perhaps, I just found it easier to be alone, and away from people yelling, fighting, and hitting on me. If that was going to be the worst of it, fine. I could handle it. Divine Purpose had another idea.

What Are Your Takeaways?

As I share my story with you, allow yourself to think back to all the things you did in order to survive. He, She or They are no longer able to hurt you. Write about what you did in order to survive. What decisions did you make? What did you tell yourself about why it was happening?

Take some time, in your sacred space, whatever that may be for you and write in your journal. Our stories were very different and our abusers were different people, the circumstances we found ourselves in were different and even though all that is true, we are very much the same in terms of what those experiences caused us to believe about ourselves and how those experiences made us feel.

Ask yourself the following questions:

1. Who were the bullies in your childhood?
2. Why do you think they did what they did to you?
3. What were your beliefs about them as a child?
4. What do you believe about them now, as an adult?

Chapter 5

WHEN DID THE GROOMING ACTUALLY BEGIN?

I QUICKLY REALIZED THAT NOT ONLY was there pain and suffering on the outside, but that the innocent, little girl I was back then had no idea of what was about to happen to her. After it all happened, and I looked back over my life's journey, I realized, just like you probably do too, most of us were "groomed" way before the actual abuse started.

I did not know what it was. I could not possibly understand it as "grooming", but only assumed this was somehow normal, and this is what Daddy's do. Nevertheless, it always felt creepy to me. It felt wrong, just plain old, wrong. I started to think about my little, innocent self, and how any of it could be happening to me. There were so many times when he would do something, say something or act in ways that even I, as a very young child, could sense as being wrong and certainly, not normal. I instinctively knew it was not at all right of him to be doing any of it. We know this to be true. Don't we? We know that while we sensed it and knew it was wrong, there was very little, if anything at all, our little selves could do about it. I understand your world. I had lived in that world for years. This is where we created our self-defense mechanisms. This is also where we started storing our Trauma. Our trauma thoughts become our beliefs about ourselves, and those beliefs about ourselves become our Identity. In essence – we get stuck in what hurt us, in what frightened us and we created emotions that caused us to forget who we truly are. More on this later in the book.

I can still see my small, innocent, and vulnerable little body. I can see him with his sick, smirky face, that sick smile, it was this grin that even as a young girl gave me the creeps every single time I saw it, and over the years, I saw it a lot. My intuition was obviously trying to warn me about something, but I was just a kid. I didn't even know what intuition was. Here are just a few examples of his grooming style.

When I was sick, it was always him and never my mother who would come into my bedroom and as I lay in my bed, a sick child, he would have that sick, smirky look on his face, because he was going to put a type of vapo-rub on my chest. Now, there's nothing wrong with a father putting ointment on his child's chest, if in fact, that is all he is doing. If his intentions are to ease his child's pain and help to make her comfortable and well again, to help her breathe better. When he's doing it because he's looking forward to all the perverted, and selfish sexual plans he has in mind for his own child, it's SICK. I was probably younger than 8-years old at the time, and I definitely did not have any breasts, but he still enjoyed himself.

Bathtime was another creepy experience for me. I would often see my mother down the hallway, which looked straight into our kitchen. She would be preparing dinner, or often she was there cleaning up after dinner. He was always the one who would help me get undressed and get into the bathtub. I was perfectly capable of getting myself undressed. I was also perfectly capable of running my own bathwater. Maybe they wanted to make sure I did not scald myself with hot water. I poured about half a bottle of bubble bath into the bathwater, so I could cover myself up with bubbles because of that creepy look on his face.

My dad always had loose change in his pant's front pockets. He would walk around the house with his hand in one of his pockets and jiggle the coins. One day I was out in the backyard, and I stepped onto a rather large cactus. I was barefoot at the time, so the pieces of cactus needles were well embedded into my foot including my toes. I could not walk and started crying out for help. My brother calls my mother and my mother calls out for my dad. He quickly picks me up and carries me over to sit on our backyard picnic table. Then, as he would often do when I had suffered an injury, to get my mind off of the pain, and as he pulled all those needles out of my foot, he told me to reach into his pocket and exclaims, quite enthusiastically, that I get to keep all the money I can pull out. I started pulling out as many coins as I could. Looking back – while it did take my mind off of the stinging, burning pain – it brought out that same creepy look on his face again.

Beginning to see a pattern here? I remember it like it happened yesterday, although the overwhelming feeling of pain and despair doesn't happen anymore. I have managed to move far past the sadness and the anxiety of it all.

Sometimes, I would try and have meaningful and heartfelt conversations with my Mother about what was happening to my growing and changing body. She had given her written permission for me to be allowed to receive the public Elementary school's course on sex education. I'm sure that's not what it was titled back then, but honestly, I don't remember what they called it. The teaching was designed to teach boys (separately from the girls) and girls (separately from the boys) in the school auditorium, about our growing, pubescent bodies. The menstrual cycle would be taught, as well as breast development, pubic changes, sanitary belts and sanitary napkins, and how to use them. Tampons were not something that was discussed. Tampons were taboo.

After that class, I would eagerly await for my *Special Time* to happen, as I checked my little-girl pubic area for hair almost daily. Then it happened! I was so excited to see something happening! It meant I was growing up! I was becoming a Woman!! I was a child who would, soon enough, be a full-fledged Woman! Woo Hoo! I thought this was the best thing that ever happened to me besides getting my first pony!

My mom would be in the kitchen cooking our dinner. I would often sit at the kitchen table watching her and I would talk with her as she cooked. On this particular day, I quietly thought to myself that this was the perfect time to get her to talk with me about what I had recently discovered. There was no way she could not give me her attention and just walk away. She was cooking dinner, so she had to stay there and listen to me and hopefully teach me something, anything about my becoming a woman! You know, she could give me the womanly guidance I was so desperately seeking and offer me her motherly support. I was looking for her undivided attention, although I knew I had to share that attention with the delicious meal she was preparing for us.

I sat there on that gray-naugahyde nook, my skinny little arms, perched, as if in prayer on our kitchen table. I was so excited. I had just found some of what I called hairs, down there, and I was really happy about my discovery! The reality of my discovery was more like pubic fuzz. Like, maybe two to four, little fuzz fluffs, but hey, it meant nature was doing it's perfect work inside my little body. I could soon tell my girlfriends at school that I was officially on my way to becoming a woman! We would soon be sharing our stories about our growing bodies, and I was excited to share! At some point in the near future I would start the long, highly anticipated Menstrual Cycle, and I would no longer be just a little girl anymore, as if that was a bad thing.

I blurted out my newfound discovery right there in our kitchen telling her that I had found hairs! Wow! I did not whisper this information, oh no, not me, I was practically singing it to high Heaven! She looked over at me, as she continued to stir whatever she had in the pot on the stove, and gave me a shy chuckle for all my naivete, as she continued to cook. I'm sure she thought it was cute and she probably thought, oh boy, is my daughter going to be let down when she starts getting menstrual cramps and has to deal with all that blood, stains on her clothing, and body bloating.

There I am telling my Mother about my new found Eureka moment! I'm so proud of my body. I'm totally in this very happy, and thrilling moment, and I'm waiting for her to give me some Motherly advice. I'm all ears, I'm leaning in, and I know it's going to be special for both of us. She has my most undivided attention. And...as I knowingly wait for this glorious, Mother and Daughter moment to blossom so beautifully, my dad walks into the open doorway of our kitchen. He was taking a nap in their bedroom, down the hall from where we were in the kitchen. He had heard me telling my mother about my pubic fluff. He decided that he would join in on the conversation.

I will never, ever, forget the feeling I had when he did

that. Remember this was before he started abusing me. He was giving me my baths for years by then, and he was already groping, and touching my sisters, but he had been waiting for me to be the right age and the right body type that he needed to get his jollies off. There's really no other way to say it. I call a spade a spade. That's just the way I AM.

He looked at me with that sick, demented smirk again, and this time it really gave me the creeps (READ: My Intuition was screaming, NO!!! LOOK OUT!!! DANGER!!! DANGER!!! RUN!!!) I remember being perturbed with him; frustrated, and thinking to myself, get out of here. What are you doing here messing up my alone time with my Mom? This is for us Females and us Females ONLY! I so desperately wanted my alone time with my Mother. I wanted him to leave us alone. This little girl had no clue what was just around the corner for her. It was going to get a whole lot worse.

I was disgusted with him. Once again, finding myself in a total state of confusion. All at once my thought's came rushing in, this is women's time. I'm well on my way to becoming a full-fledged woman, and you are not invited to the party! No boys or men with Penises allowed! It really bothered me. I had no idea how bad it was all going to get after that evening. I thought I was just bugged because he imposed himself into our private conversation, and interrupted our special, Mother and Daughter time together. Oh, boy!! Was I ever wrong? He had much more sinister plans for me in mind, and I was just letting him know that the proverbial forbidden fruit was almost ripe for the taking.

My mom looks over at him, and I can literally feel her energy shift. She's shyly chuckling at me one moment and then the next she's looking at him with a double-shot of disdain followed by a heartbreak-chaser. I saw it. I definitely felt it. I just did not understand what it was that I was witnessing.

That was truly the beginning of the end for me. This was the moment that marks my five and a half years of almost daily emotional, sometimes physical and always sexual abuse by the man who was supposed to protect me from all others. My God, what that does to an innocent child's psyche. Oh, the damage done. It is a miracle that all abused children don't commit suicide, because the suffering is extremely intense. Words can barely express adequately just how painful our little bodies feel. If we do not receive the extensive care we require, our young minds struggle for the rest of our lives to overcome the damage done. Many of us have little to no support. We struggle daily with overwhelming feelings of shame, guilt, fear and heartbreaking unworthiness. More so than not, we usually suffer in silence, and we always feel alone – completely and utterly alone. Life, from this point forward, became my own personal Mount Everest to survive.

He made some weird joke about me and I don't even remember exactly how he said it, or what he said. I do remember that he was obviously there because he was letting my mother know that daughter #3 was almost ready for the taking. She never had the strength or the courage to stand up to him and protect her daughters. She wasn't a mean mother. She was very loving in her own ways. She was not expressive, she did not say I Love You to her children like I have always said to mine, but we were loved.

Everything she did was for her children. She worked for us kids, she cooked, cleaned, did tons of laundry, hung clothes out to dry on the clothesline before my dad finally bought her a dryer. At some point, she delegated house chores. I would pick up dog poop and feed our family dog her breakfast and dinner. I would dust and polish the furniture. I would clean the kitchen sink after dinner, wash the dishes and put them away. I would clean our bathroom. I would clean my room and keep it tidy. Sometimes, I would have dinner ready for her before she got home from work. Okay, granted, it was usually T-bone Steak, Tater Tots and canned corn, but it meant dinner was served and she did not have to come home from a hard day's work and have to cook dinner for us.

I received an allowance from my dad weekly, so I did have an incentive to do a good job, but mostly, I felt proud to be contributing to our family, and to help my mother who did so much for the family she loved. I think, maybe deep down I must have been feeling sorry for her. Somehow I knew she carried a heavy burden. I did not feel anger toward her yet, but that was about to change.

I had absolutely no clue about the looming danger that awaited me just around the bend. It was a time long before the renowned "Just Say No" campaign had made its debut. Although this campaign primarily aimed to combat alcohol and drug abuse, it also empowered children to confidently assert their refusal by uttering a simple two-letter word: NO! Moreover, these events unfolded several decades prior to the courageous Oprah Winfrey publicly sharing the painful ordeals she endured in her childhood. I AM forever grateful for your profound bravery, Oprah.

In order for me to write this book, I consciously chose to take a look back, and in retrospect, I wondered, what was worse. The selfish sexually abusive acts my father did to me, or the fact that he messed with my innocent, little mind? Bruises can heal, the stings of being whipped by a belt can stop stinging, or being hit over the head with the shoes I left in the living room instead of putting them away in my room where they belonged; even the touching and groping of my private parts would eventually stop, but the gaslighting, the lies, the threats, the brainwashing that caused me to lose my Mother's love, is by far, the worst card I could have ever been dealt. I loved my mother. I needed my mother. I needed my mother to love me. I craved her love. I certainly craved her attention. I wanted her to be proud of me.

Not only did my father take what was not his to take from his daughter in a physical sense, I believe that my relationship with my mother never flourished in the way it could have. It was strained and it was tested. It would come very close to almost being completely destroyed as a direct result of his actions. Not only was I raped and abused sexually, but his actions nearly killed any chance I had of experiencing the Mother-Daughter relationship that my mother and I could have embraced together for the rest of our lives. I lost my Father. I came close to losing my Mother. I definitely Lost My Innocence. I nearly lost my mind, and all of it nearly cost me my life.

What Are Your Takeaways?

As I continue to share my story with you, now you can allow yourself to think back to all the things you did in order to survive. He, She or They are no longer able to hurt you. Write about what you did in order to survive. What decisions did you make? What did you tell yourself about why it was happening?

Remember to take some long, slow, deep breaths. Now is the time to write in your journal. Ask yourself the following questions:

1. Do you remember any grooming being done to you as a child?
2. Write as much as you can remember about those experiences. It's okay, they cannot hurt you now. You are safe.
3. Do you see how you were overpowered not only physically, but mentally and emotionally? There was nothing you could have done to stop it.

Chapter 6

FEAR OF LOSING MY MOM AND OTHER LIES I WAS TOLD

I WAS LIED TO PROBABLY A hundred times a day for most of my childhood, if not all of it. That's what it felt like, anyway. The worst thing my father told me was that my mother would not love me anymore if she found out about what "we" were doing, (as if I was making the choice to participate with him) and **she would stop loving me**. As child abuse survivors, we struggle with the pack of lies we were forced to hear about ourselves. This chapter is creating the space for you, my Dear Readers, to acknowledge all those lies that you too, were told. They happened, and none of us are alone when it comes to all those lies that have hurt us. What must ultimately matter to you now, is being aware of what those lies cost you, and will continue to cost you today and for all your tomorrows, if you choose to hold onto them.

There is a difference between acknowledging that we were lied to and not owning the lies. If there is anything this book underscores, it's the fact that we are not the sum of all the terrible things that happened to us in our past. We are so much more than that! I AM Saying this to you again, my Dear Sweet Reader, **You Are Not the Sum of All the Terrible Things that Happened in Your Past. You are so much more than that! You Must Remember Who You Are.**

Someone was taken away from me. A young girl of 16 years old, abused or not, needs her mother. It should have been my mother who taught me about my growing body. It should have been my mother who taught me about menstruation, and instead it was my school's health education program where I learned about getting my first period. School! That's really up close and personal. The public school system takes on the responsibility and the authority of what, in my most humble opinion, should be a parent's duty. What should be the parents' duties or the child's legal guardians' duties and responsibilities should, again, in my experience and personal opinion, not be in the hands of the public school system, or any other school system for that matter.

My mother was able to go shopping with me and teach me about wearing a bra, so that's some great Mother and Child bonding for you. That's about it. Nothing about boys, nothing about babies, at least not until after my first child was born, nothing about abortion, nothing about taking the pill, or as my school principal used to say, nothing said about how "holding hands leads to sexual intercourse." My dad was right about one thing, she was very shy and uncomfortable talking about these topics. I believe, to this day, that he used her shyness, her inability to talk with me about the *facts of life*, and all those *birds and those bees* definitely flew the nest. He knew what he looked forward to and planned. All of it became his perfect excuse to continue grooming me and get inside my head so he could eventually get inside my body.

We Go Into Fight, Flight or Freeze Mode

It will be forever etched in my mind's eye. My father on top of me, in my parents' bedroom, and me laying underneath him, I was completely frozen. I was an 11 year old girl completely naked, and I barely batted an eye, yet tears were streaming down my face.

I glanced over at my Mother's dresser, my Mother was a practicing Catholic. She had statues of Saints, and some photos of religious people. I didn't know who they were, or what they meant to her but I believed they were powerful. They had Halos over their heads, so I knew they had to be very powerful. I distinctly remember looking at them and thinking WHY AREN'T YOU HELPING ME? I remember thinking, YOU ARE SAINTS, you are able to stop my Father from doing this BAD, Disgusting Thing to me! PLEASE HELP ME! PLEASE MAKE HIM STOP. Quietly, in my mind I was begging for mercy. I was calling on the Saints, the Angels, The Virgin Mary, Herself; and her Son, Jesus Christ, to intervene and stop my dad from what he was doing to me. But nobody did. Nothing changed. No Saints, No Virgin Mary. No JESUS, NO GOD Intervened. No INNOCENT CHILD WAS SAVED that day, or any of those days and years that followed.

That abuse happened almost daily, every time I came home from school. It happened in my parents bedroom, my bedroom, in my parents bathroom, in their shower, and sometimes when I was alone in the car with him.

How could it be that nobody saw the signs? I started rebelling. I started acting out. I couldn't be bothered with schoolwork. I loved English class, physical education class, my dog and my pony. I loved my Mother, my two older sisters and my two older brothers. I loved my friends.

That was almost the beginning of the end for me.

When anyone suffers from a traumatic event it is extremely difficult to move forward. I don't have to convince you of that, you have lived it, or you are reading this book because you know someone who is a survivor. You know all too well what that experience does to our young and completely innocent minds and bodies.

My hope, my wish for you, is that if you learn anything from this book, it is that You LEARN that You Do Matter. You Do Deserve Love. You Did Not Do A Damn Thing to Deserve Any of It. It happened, it was heartbreaking, horrific, and disgusting. Now, You must Allow YOURSELF to HEAL! Read every book you can get your hands on. Go to therapy if that is something you feel will help you. Never neglect your spiritual self. For God's Sake, go to church if you want to worship. Go out in nature, walk along the beach, or wherever you feel close to Nature/God. Go to group therapy, if you choose. Attend seminars, workshops, take courses, get a Life Coach who specializes in Trauma Recovery, Empowerment, and has experience with being abused, themself. Educate yourself and act on that education to better heal yourself and your life. It gets better. You have no idea how quickly your life can become better, and if you run away and give up too soon, because you tell yourself you cannot take the suffering any longer, you will have given up too soon. Life gets better and it is through your pain and suffering that you build Resilience. Never, ever, give up on yourself and never give up on Life.

We were too young to do anything about all of these lies, all of this affected our minds and our bodies. Your body/ mind is not two separate entities, they are actually one, i.e., one unit working together.

This could not have been made more clear to me than on the day my mother came home from work unexpectedly. Apparently, she walked home from her bus stop because she had left something she needed for work at home. She thought my dad was away at work, and I would be home alone, but he had left for work, and then he came back home. There were no cell phones back then. No texting. She did not call the house phone to let me know she was on her way.

My dad had already started his sexual exploits on me this particular morning. He had me in their bedroom, in their bed. Picture this if you dare, my dad has me, now at about 12 years old, in my parents bed. He hears the front door being opened, grabs his pants, and tells me to say I wasn't feeling good, so I climbed in bed with him. My mother walks into her bedroom and she stands past the now opened door looking at us both. She knew he was home because his car was parked in front of our house. I believe she knew what she was witnessing. How could she not? I have no doubt that she wanted to protect me and put an end to this. She simply did not know how to end it all. She rather calmly, and almost stoically, asks him, "what are you doing?" He replies, by nodding at me. That was my clue. I am supposed to tell her that I was not feeling well, and I asked to climb into their bed which was somehow going to make me feel better. Not only did he sexually, emotionally and physically abuse me, he also blamed it all on me. He led her to believe that it was all my idea. How sick is that?

Babies, toddlers, teenagers, males and females all become chattel. Lust, sex, violence, drugs, and money, avalanches of money and greed take center stage and Evil, aka, Egoic Mind, takes control of one's mind, heart and spirit. These harbingers of darkness threaten to corrupt and tarnish the purest of souls. Innocent lives are being lost because of those ensnared by greed. I will never be a person who supports not calling Pedophiles exactly what they are, PEDOPHILES! Never will I call a pedophile a Minor-Attracted Person. NEVER!

Consequently, the insidious form of Evil, better known as Egoic Mind, seizes control, commandeering the fragile sanctuaries of the mind, heart, and soul. In such a troubling landscape, it is vital that we confront the truth with unyielding determination. As a steadfast advocate for justice and protection of the innocent, I condemn any complicity in obscuring the reality of despicable predators. It is my unwavering conviction that we must unequivocally brand those who prey upon minors with the stark name they rightfully deserve: Pedophiles. This unflinching identification allows us to address the issue head-on, to foster awareness, and to take decisive action against this reprehensible crime. Together, we must stand united in our pursuit for a world free from the clutches of such cowardice and greed.

Nothing happened. How could it be that nothing happened? This goes on all the time in families. It has to stop! Many decades later, my mother and I had a phone conversation. I was still attempting to get her to admit that she was told, in fact, by my oldest sister and me exactly what she saw that day, and what he had been doing to her daughters for years. Her response was like a punch to my gut. She replied, "What did it matter, you were already doing things with other boys, anyway?" My reaction was one of shock. Her words literally knocked the wind out of me. I dropped the phone. I could not believe she had just said this to her own daughter, and after all these years. I quickly picked up the phone, and said to her, "Even if that were true, Mom, which it was not, how would it justify my father sexually abusing me for years?"

I did not want to hurt her. I did not want to cause her any more pain. I only wanted her to know the truth. I wanted her to understand that none of it was my idea. I hated every perverted moment of it. I would have much rather spent every one of those painful moments in which I was forced to be his sexual slave – just being a happy, young child, who was free to go play outside with her friends. To be free to walk home from school happy, turn on the TV and watch my beloved cartoons. I would have chosen to spend time with my mother, my dog, my pony, listen to music, dance and sing and be with my friends.

This is what happens when we live in denial. This is what happens when we are not honest with ourselves and with others. These are the types of abuses that happen the entire world over, when we are ruled by our Egoic minds.

In my Not so humble opinion, I believe that children are having sex far too young. Stop and look at that sentence I just typed. The words *"Children"* and *"are having sex"* should never be in the same sentence! Have people lost their minds? Some obviously have. We have lost our National virginity, so to speak, and far too soon.

The issues of teen pregnancy, abortion, and even divorce, as well as childhood and domestic abuse, could be quelled much better if we stopped looking at freedom as a means to shirk our responsibilities as parents. I believe we can do better. We need to do better as parents, as guardians, as individuals, as communities, and as human beings. We must raise our standards. We must level ourselves up if we ever want to see the numbers of victims decline.

Human sex-trafficking and sexual exploitation are growing in numbers.[2] Thank God for Tim Ballard.[3] Thank God for the beautiful Soul who is Jim Cavizal and for

---

[2] "Operation Underground Railroad - Wikipedia." https://en.wikipedia.org/wiki/Operation_Underground_Railroad. Accessed 23 Jun. 2023.

[3] "Operation Underground Railroad and the Fight to End Modern Day ...." https://www.imdb.com/title/tt9397842/. Accessed 23 Jun. 2023.

all those brave souls who are Operation Underground Railroad, and so many others; those caring, unselfish, non-profits, good people spending time, energy and money, not to mention putting their own lives at risk, to help save the Innocent Children of the World.

Thank God for Angel Studios, for having the fortitude to produce and distribute *Sound of Freedom* not for how many millions the film can make, but for the *Awareness* the film will create in those who watch it. We must pay attention and protect the most vulnerable – the world's Children. While I was not trafficked, I do know, all too well, what it felt like to be a slave for sex in my own home for many years; that is, until I grew strong enough to save myself. These children are not able to run away. They are often trafficked to other countries, they know nothing about. They are chained, locked up, sexually abused and they are starved nearly to death.

Do your homework. For me, this is not a political issue. This is a Human Rights Issue. Children must never be used as pawns for political agendas. Take the time to thoroughly investigate, educate yourselves, evaluate and delve into what is truly unfolding in your country, as well as on a global scale. It is imperative that we recognize and acknowledge the existence of certain individuals who actively promote their own personal agendas, even within the realm of politics. Shockingly, it is alleged that in some countries there are instances where children as young as 3-years of age are being advocated to possess the *legal capacity to consent to engaging in sexual acts with adults*. Most 3-year olds can't even spell C-O-N-S-E-N-T, let alone give it! Such a notion is profoundly disturbing to me and it raises vital questions about any society that believes these absurdities. I highly question its moral compass.

What Are Your Takeaways?

That was a tough chapter to write. I know it was difficult for you to read. It needs to be said. We must have these difficult conversations. Children are not chattel. They are innocent and they are not strong enough in body/mind to protect themselves from the Evil that walks this planet. We must not only care about our own painful childhood experiences, but we must also care about all children everywhere. Together we can pray for their safety. Together we can meditate on and visualize their protection from harm. We must be their Saving Grace!!

Take some time, in your sacred space. Ask yourself the following questions:

1. Were you lied to?
2. Who lied to you?
3. What were the lies he/she/they told you?
4. How did those lies you were told shape your beliefs about yourself back then?
5. How long did you hold onto those beliefs about yourself?
6. What do you believe about yourself as an adult, now?

Chapter 7
FINDING WAYS TO ESCAPE AND SURVIVE

$\mathcal{H}$OW DOES THE SAYING GO? "When life gives you lemons, you make lemonade."

No matter what happens to us in life, we always have the power to make decisions that can change our destiny. I chose to make one of the most important decisions of my entire life when I was only 16. In order to avoid being available to him, and thus, not be sexually abused by my father and to protect myself from further abuse, I started thinking in terms of a way out. It did not always work, but even as a young girl, I was beginning to gain survival skills. I share with you now how I started planning and watching the hours, days and weeks of my life tick away.

Over the years, we started growing up. We started getting stronger and wiser. This is where we start to think in terms of stopping it, asking for help, telling someone or maybe even running away from home. In order to not be there for my father when he got home from work, I quickly ran the 1.5 miles home from school, threw my school books down and grabbed a snack. Then I took off as fast as I could, while watching for his car. I ran to my friend's house a good 3 blocks away from home. I would often stay at my friend's house until I knew my mother was back home, after he had picked her up at her bus stop. Then, and only then, would I feel safe enough to return to that house.

Childhood abuse survivors share one thing in common. While it is very difficult for many of us to talk about what happened, it is a process – it is a journey, and we do want to talk about it. We all need a Witness. We want to be heard. We want to be acknowledged, and understood for what we went through in our lives. My goal here is to give you the space to do this, without reliving your past. Your past is not who you really are. It is over and done with. You are so much more than all that stuff that happened back then. None of it has any true power over you anymore, except for the power that you give to it.

If there is anything this book underscores, it is the fact that we are not the sum of all the terrible things that happened to us in our past. We are so much more than that.

To add insult to injury, my dad would play mind games of the worse kind. If I was outside trying to avoid seeing him when he wanted me to be home and thus available to him, he would pick fights with my mom and whatever brother or sister was nearby. It was like walking on broken glass with him. I experienced a significant amount of stress because I worried, constantly, over what personality he would be wearing on any given day, at any given moment. Was he going to be a Dr. Jekyll or a Mr. Hyde? Either way, he was still a Pedophile.

What Are Your Takeaways?

Okay, you know the drill. Breathe slowly, deeply, and get yourself quiet and calm. When you are ready, ask yourself the following questions:

1. Write about what you did to escape the abuse. It may be that you were unable to do anything at all. That's okay. You were too young to fight back. None of it was ever your fault. Stop beating yourself up for the things you could not do to stop it.
2. Were you able to tell anyone what was happening or what had happened?
3. Did anyone try to save you?
4. What does the Adult you are Now feel?

Chapter 8

SHE'S LEAVING HOME, BYE-BYE

*A*FTER 5+ YEARS OF SEXUAL abuse by my father, and trying to hide from him at my friend's home after school no longer worked, I decided to try yet another strategy. I'm now in the 10th grade, in my first semester of High School and I'm very angry. Being a teenager can be a difficult time in a person's life, being a teenager who has been repeatedly emotionally, physically and sexually abused for years, is almost a death sentence. It can certainly prove to be a suicide sentence. I finally told my best friend about what he was doing to me, and she was furious. I can still remember her words as if it were yesterday. Rather adamantly she exclaimed, "We have got to get you out of there!" I will also always remember my reaction to her response. Her caring words were truly music to my ears. While I did not actually speak these words out loud to her, this is what I thought. *You mean, I'm Actually Worth Saving?* And, *My Life Really Does Matter?* Together, we forged a plan of action. Our only goal was to get me out of that house. The plan was for me to run away from home. This was a critical moment on my journey of survival.

What a sad plan it was... I must run away from the only home I had ever known. My friend set up the plan with her two older sisters and their boyfriends. They all liked to party and smoke pot, among other things. One of the guys had recently been arrested for robbery and selling pot. He was facing some time in prison. I didn't really know much about any of that. I would need to sneak out while my parents were away at work and never come back to that house of horrors. I had no control over anything to do with my running away, except to get myself out of that house.

I'm not sure if I lost my mother early on during the beginning of the abuse, or on the day I made the decision to run away from home. Either way, someone else was taken away from me. I remember feeling so afraid. I did not want to leave home, but it was the only hope I had of protecting myself from his continued abuse. I was petrified with the fear that my mother would find out. I could not lose her. Leaving my mom, my dog, my pony and my friends was the only choice I had. It was a choice, a decision, that hurt like Hell.

Since I was a huge Beatles fan, I said to myself, "Maybe my mom will figure it out if I play *She's Leaving Home,* by The Beatles. Yeah! That's it! She will figure it out! Then he will be stopped and he will be the one who has to leave; and not me. I will be saved, and I won't have to run away from home."

I painstakingly played that song on my record player over and over and over again. I sang the words, I cried, and nobody noticed my cry for help. When Paul McCartney sings, *"Daddy, our baby's gone."* I felt so sad, it was excruciatingly painful. I knew it was going to really hurt my mother, and the last thing I wanted to cause her was more pain.

She was going to worry herself sick, and it would all be my fault. I sat there in my bedroom, all alone. I was shaking from the stress, the worry, and the fears of what was going to happen next once I left home. I thought about all the good times, and all the fun I had way back when, before all of the abuse and grooming had started. My little-girl self was so confident back then, completely tenacious, high-spirited, and happy. Now, the teenager I had become was trembling at the ugly reality of the decision she had to make. With The Beatles singing, *She's Leaving Home*, I quietly curled up in the fetal position and cried myself to sleep.

The infamous, terrifying day finally arrives. I gather up my belongings while my best friend and her sister wait in the car parked in front of our home. Sobbing, I hug my beautiful, loving Dog, Terry. I'm heartbroken with having to leave her. Shaking like a leaf, I rush out of the house. They drive to their house several miles away. This will be the first place my parents will look for me, once they realize that I have run away. Quickly, after that first stop, I'm taken to the apartment of my friend's sister's friend. I stay in the spare bedroom. There was a TV in the room, and a twin bed. I had some snacks that I brought with me and a little bit of clothing stuffed into a gym bag that I had sewn in Jr. High school. Whatever the man and woman I stayed with ate for dinner, I was given some to eat, too. I am shaking with fear, and while my best friend does stay with me on my first day there, eventually she must leave and go home and then go back to school. She keeps her silence as to my whereabouts.

My mother was heartbroken. Approximately 2 weeks later, my oldest brother was given the telephone number for where I was hiding out. He said something like, "You better get your ass back home now! Mom is very worried about you. She nearly had a heart attack! She had to go to the hospital, and she's walking around now with a heart monitor on. You Get Your Ass Back Home Now!!" He also spoke of how my father had gone to my highschool and was literally looking in dumpsters and in street gutters for my body. My brother was furious with me. He simply did not know the Truth. I was far too afraid to tell him why I had left home.

I could not tell him why I had run away. I froze. I did not think he would believe me. Back then, most people were quick to label child abuse victims as liars. They did not know what to do upon hearing such information. When Oprah Winfrey went public with her story, people finally started to pay attention. Oprah bravely opened the lines of communication, she gave victims of child sexual abuse a much needed voice. I offer Oprah my gratitude for boldly daring to share publicly her own truth.

Tears were, once again, streaming down my face. All I could think about was my mother, and how terribly I had hurt her. My entire body shook in fear. My Mother's heart was not the only heart in our family that was close to breaking. I felt completely alone. I missed my mother, I missed my family, I missed my dog. My pony had already been sold by this time because I was getting too big for him. I wanted to come home, but I wanted my dad to leave that house.

My Uncle was working as a Private Eye back then. He offered to help my parents in their search for me. I stayed in this apartment for about a month, before my Uncle worked out a deal with the "kidnappers." They gathered up my stuff, and took me to a place where we waited for my Uncle to arrive. Apparently, my Uncle was able to work out some sort of parole deal with the lawyers involved regarding the crimes these guys had committed. I was the catalyst for that. They agreed to give me back to my Uncle, in exchange, in the hopes of a shortened jail sentence. My Uncle took me back to his home and I stayed there with him and his wife for about two weeks, until it was decided to bring me back home.

As I walked back into my home my mother hugged me.

My oldest sister was close by my side. My other sister was non-existent. My brothers were not there either. My father kept his distance. He stayed in their bedroom. He did not come out to greet me, nor did he say anything to me. I was exhausted, just from the stress of it all. I stayed in my bedroom. Once again, I curled up in the fetal position and wept alone. It was just me with my records and my Terry dog and my Teddy Bear, sad, frightened and confused.

A few days after my return, my mother came in and told me to take a pill she was holding in her hand. She said it was a truth serum and it would make me tell the Truth about why I ran away. I remember being asked questions by her. I don't think I felt any real effects of whatever pill it was she gave me. All I wanted to do was to cry and to sleep. You could feel the tension in that house. My father continued to not say a word to me, nor I to him.

On one particular morning, my oldest sister came in and told me we were going for a drive in her car with our mother. She did not tell me why. As she drove us far away from that house, my mother in the passenger seat, and I in the back seat, my sister drove us ever so carefully, and she started to explain to me why we were doing this. She carefully looked over her right shoulder at me as she drove, she asked me to tell our mother why I ran away from home. She assured me that I was not in any trouble, and I would not be punished for anything I said. She told me that she had already talked with our mother and that she had already informed our mother about some of the things our father had done to her. She tried to reassure me that it was okay for me to tell, in my own words, what our father was doing to me before I chose to run away.

Talk about being afraid! I was almost numb with fear. I certainly trusted my oldest sister. I knew firsthand that she had tried her best to save me way before this point in time. There was a time when I was alone at home and my father was there. He had me go into our living room and sit on our sofa, where he often told me to go, knowing my mother was far away working. He would often take Polaroid photos of me topless in the living room. He would have me pose for the photos. This was far before cell phones, the internet and personal computers were invented. He had that Poloroid camera, and he loved it, apparently, more than he loved me.

He was just getting started with me, and then I heard a sound at our front door. It was my sister trying to get into the house, so he quickly jumped up and left me there on the sofa. He ran to the door, and they started yelling at each other. Again, I froze. I hoped this time I would be saved.

My father was 6' 2", and in quite good shape back then. He was very strong, and healthy. My sister, on the other hand, was taller than I was, but she was not very strong, physically. She was rather slim and much weaker. She confronts him telling him that she knows what he's up to, and he won't get away with it. She knows what he's doing right there to me, at that very moment.

I don't move except to lean forward, put my top back on and peek out enough to see the two of them arguing back and forth. He's angry, very, very angry! She tries her best to come inside the house, but he's much stronger than she is and he's yelling at her to leave and never come back. She's pushing forward and he's pushing her outward. Her voice was trembling.

My oldest sister never got into any confrontations with my parents. She was good. She was kind. Here she was standing up to him, this monster of a man. I was so proud of her for trying to stop him. I'm so grateful to her for loving me, and risking what she did to try to save me. She tells him she's going to tell our mother, and the very last thing I hear him say to her is "If you do, I'll kill you!!! Get Out!!" Then he slams the door in her terrified face.

My beautiful, sweet, loving sister. She passed away many years later from Breast Cancer. I have always believed that he was the reason she left us far too soon. Unresolved feelings can fester and brew in our body/minds creating illness and disease much later in life. I'm no doctor, I'm no scientist, I'm somebody who has witnessed it as it happened. I know what toll it took on my health, and I witnessed what it did to her.

She is defeated. I don't know what she did after that. I could not see her. He continued with me on the family sofa, just where he left off. He acted as if nothing had just happened. Except to say that she was stupid. We were always called stupid. Hey, Dad, Stupid Is As Stupid Does. Sadly, I was not saved that day either. I just ended up being even more confused.

There in her car with my mother finally interested in what her daughters were trying so desperately to tell her, I spoke. I told my truth. I answered all of their questions. There it was done. All those years of keeping it all locked away deep within my heart and mind. It was out. Now, he was going to get his just rewards. Now he was going to have to leave us alone for once and for all. I was finally saved!

Stopping the abuse was what I wanted, to say the least, but leaving my mom, and my dog? I did not want to do that. All I ever wanted was to tell my mom. I wanted her to save me. I wanted her to choose me over him. I wanted her to protect me. I wanted her to tell me she loved me and nothing could ever change that. I wanted her to hold me tight in her loving arms and wipe my tears away. None of those things I wanted, so desperately, ever happened. I don't know why she could not save me. Maybe, just maybe, she wasn't supposed to?

The antidote for the problem of what to do with Wild Child, Marie, was simple. Take her out of that house.

What Are Your Takeaways?

Breathe, and center yourself. Give yourself some well deserved gratitude for all the work you are doing for yourself. When you are ready, ask yourself the following questions:

1. Did you do anything to escape? If yes, what did you do? There are no right or wrong answers here.
2. Write down all you can remember about how you started growing-up and what you were able to do or not do to protect yourself and make it all stop.
3. Did anybody believe you?
4. Did anyone save you?
5. How do you feel about that Now, as an Adult?

Chapter 9
LET'S RECAP AS FOLLOWS

- I have been growing up in a very dysfunctional family environment that I thought was perfectly normal.
- I was being groomed by my father starting from at least 5 or 6 years of age although I was far too young to know what grooming was.
- I developed Asthma and had become ill with Double Pneumonia before I reached puberty. Stress related, no doubt.
- I found solace in nature and especially with dogs, ponies, horses and bunnies. I was becoming highly sensitive. I was born an Empath and yet I did not know that Empath's exist. We are, in fact, very real, and very gifted.
- My father was my Hero and also my worst Enemy.
- My mother was helpless to protect me and keep me safe from harm.

- At age 11 my father told me that my mother was very shy and couldn't talk with me about sex, boys or even my growing body. He had taken on the added responsibility of teaching me himself. He told me that he had to do all of this for her and for me.
- I'm sworn to secrecy, believing that if I told my mother what my father was doing, she would be upset and very angry with me. He told me she would not believe me, and she would stop loving me forever. Forever is a very long time.
- I have been used as a sex slave in my own home, by my biological father for many years. He deliberately picks fights, for no apparent reason, with my Mom, and siblings. I told myself that he did this because I was not home and I did not make myself available to him after he was home from work. He was very angry at me, and my family suffered for it.
- Dad played mind games, like threatening to put my dog to sleep when there was nothing wrong with her, and selling my pony so I would understand that I had to be home and available to him at all times.
- On one particular morning, my mom walked in and saw us together, in their bed, and then she went back to work. He drives her this time. He instructed me in what I had to say to her as being the reason we were together. I was not saved. Nothing changed.
- I believed God must no longer love me; otherwise, why would all this be happening to me? The belief that God no longer loved me stayed with me for many decades.
- After many years of abuse, I confided in my best friend, and together we planned my escape.
- I reluctantly ran away from home at 16 in an attempt to stop being sexually abused.

- My parents found out where I was staying and eventually I was taken back home. The thought of going back home absolutely terrified me.
- My oldest sister tries to get me to explain to our mother the real reasons for my running away. I was not, in fact, just a rebellious teenager.
- My mother painstakingly listens to my reasons, although it's too much for her to handle. She's obviously stressed and frustrated and overwhelmed.
- My mother and father decide it's best for everyone in the family that I move out of our home and be placed with my oldest sister in Granada Hills, CA, approximately 10 miles from what used to be my home.

$\mathcal{M}$Y OLDEST SISTER WAS ALWAYS more like a mother figure to me, because of our age difference and also because she was a kind and very nurturing Soul. She was loving, generous and very sweet. She was also very introverted. Most likely because of the abuse my father had done and due to receiving very little support from our mother. I moved in with my sister in her 2-bedroom apartment. This is the second time I must leave my mother, my dog and my home, as if the first time wasn't difficult enough. No pets were allowed at the apartment complex, otherwise, I would have taken Terry with me.

High School was just a couple of blocks down the street from the apartment, so I could walk to and from school. Since I didn't know how to drive a car yet, and I didn't have my driver's license, this works out just fine. Within a few months my sister had taught me how to drive in her yellow, Volkswagen Beetle. I passed my driver's behind the wheel testing and the DMV written test. When my sister is home and she has no plans to go out, she graciously allows me to use her car to go see friends, etc. Quickly I made some new friends, and soon drove us all to the beach.

My mother thought it was a good idea to buy me another horse. I agreed with her wholeheartedly. We saw an ad in the local newspaper where a Strawberry Roan, Arabian Horse was up for sale up past Lake View Terrace, near Hansen Dam. There was a summer camp for children with disabilities there, and they were attempting to ride this horse. Troy was his name, he was full of energy. He rarely walked, mostly he cantered, galloped and ran. My sister drove my mother there to check him out. I rode double with my best friend on her Morgan Horse, all the way up to near Hansen Dam. If we wanted to buy the horse, I would ride him back home. Troy was a very high-spirited horse. He was an Arabian, and Arabian Horses are very high-spirited animals. The owners just wanted him to go to a good home, after they realized Troy was far too much horse for the children to try to ride. It was not safe for them. For me, on the other hand, I loved his high-spirited energy. I wanted him and fell in love with him right on the spot! My mom agreed and signed on the dotted line. I rode him home to the place where I would board him. Troy was an absolutely beautiful horse. I miss him. Eventually, I found a place where I could board him closer to the apartment in Granada Hills. I was happy. I would ride all the time, when I wasn't in school.

I was doing alright, until I met him. He was really cute, all the girls in school liked him. He was a rebel, which of course made me even more attracted to him. What the hell did I know, I was a teenage girl who had already been molested for years and abused by her very own father, so I was definitely behaving like a Rebel.

Everything happened so quickly. This boyfriend of mine, I'll call him Stu. He was a year older than I was. We became boyfriend and girlfriend, as in going steady. We are definitely having sex. I'm a Rebel too, after all, and it's pissing my father off that I'm having sex with someone other than him. The pill did not work so well for me though. A few months into our *courtship*, I became pregnant. My parents were both furious. Imagine that. Neither one of them did a wonderful job at raising me. My mother was unsuccessful at protecting me from my dad, but I was, yet again, the problem child because I got pregnant.

They both insisted that I get an abortion. Abortion had just become legal in the state of California. Although, having an abortion was not something I wanted to do. I wanted to keep my baby. Afterall, the baby would be mine and nobody could ever take him/her away from me.

If you have never been through taking the life of that little blob, the spark of Light already making its connection inside of your womb who will eventually become a little human being, I highly suggest that you don't. Unless you have no conscience at all, it is a terrifying, gut-wrenching experience. My parents told me that I was underage, and because I was not an adult yet, I must do what they said. I believed them. Remember, I was *stupid.*

After high school we eventually married in Tijuana, Mexico. I was underage, but my mother wrote me a letter which gave me her permission to cross the US/Mexico border out of San Diego, CA and get married. Yes, it was just that easy to cross the border at 17. Approximately 9 months later our son was born.

My boyfriend and I really just wanted to live together but my mom said my father would be furious if we did that, so we had to get married. It cost us maybe $28 to be married in T.J. After we split up it cost me hundreds of dollars to get a divorce and prove myself a fit mother. My soon to be Ex-husband's mother decided she wanted him to sue me for custody of our son. I won full custody of my son. My ex had visitation rights, although he rarely used them. He had quickly developed a drinking problem. It's sad really, he was a nice person when he wasn't drinking. He grew up with dysfunctional parents, his sister was an addict and his older brother was a hardcore addict. His father died due to alcoholism. We had many battles over visitation and child support, which I almost never received. I was always watching to make sure he was not drinking anywhere near my son. Many times, the terrible actions that human beings inflict upon each other are only surpassed by the terrible actions they inflict upon themselves. These problems arise when our Egoic Minds take control of us.

What Are Your Takeaways?

As I share my story with you, allow yourself to think back to all the things you did in order to survive. He, She or They are no longer able to hurt you. Write about what you did in order to survive. What decisions did you make? What did you tell yourself about why it was happening?

Take some time, in your sacred space and write in your journal. Our stories were very different and our abusers were different people, the circumstances we found ourselves in were different. Even though all this is true, we are very much the same in terms of what those experiences caused us to believe about ourselves and how those experiences made us feel. Do the work, and ask yourself the following questions:

1. Did your school grades suffer as a result of the abuse? Or, did you decide you had to be an even better person, and get better grades in school?
2. Have you been holding onto guilt because of the choices you made?
3. What happened to your relationships, i.e., family, friends, neighbors?
4. Now that you are an Adult, how are your relationships?

Chapter 10

MOTHER NATURE'S SON

*M*Y BEAUTIFUL, BOUNCING BABY BOY was born just two and a half months after my 18th birthday. He was born healthy, and he was absolutely perfect! I had a whole lot to learn about breastfeeding, changing diapers and babies spitting up. I loved every moment of being a new mom. I was very young to be a mother responsible for another human being. No matter how much I loved him, I was far too young, but I did the very best that I could. Would I have made better decisions back then if I knew then what I know now? Would I have not become a mother at 18 in the first place if my dad had not sexually, emotionally and physically abused me? Probably not, but then the world would be deprived of the wonderful man who is my son. I can no longer beat myself up for some of the ignorant decisions I made back when I was an abused teenage girl with a newborn baby.

When I was eight months pregnant with my son, my beloved companion, our family dog passed away. My brother called me and asked me to drive over to the house.

My entire family knew I loved Terry and I would not take the news well. They also knew I was a month away from giving birth and they did not know what that shocking news would do to me. I quickly got myself ready and drove to the house. My brother had been crying, he loved that beautiful sweet dog, my entire family loved her, even our father. For all his faults and the demons he struggled with, probably for most of his life, my father had a very soft spot for animals. Especially our beloved Terry. We had her from the time she was just a pup, and she lived well past 17. I grew up with her, as I was just barely a 1-year old when my oldest sister received Terry as a gift from our parents.

When I was old enough to pitch in and help with the household chores it was my responsibility to feed Terry, take her for walks, pick up her poop, and give her baths and grooming, all of which I hugely enjoyed. Anytime she had to go for a Veterinarian appointment, I was there. I held onto her and I comforted her, no matter what. I Love Animals. The Empath in me has always had a very special connection with animals.

But, I digress…Stu, was away at work, in downtown Los Angeles. He would be out of the apartment (we shared the apartment with my older brother) and he would catch a commuter bus to L.A. very early in the morning. I would pick him up at the bus stop in the evening after his work day. We only had one car, and I needed it in order to drive to all my OB appointments, do the grocery shopping, and run errands. He would go to sleep early in the evening so he could get up early to go to work the following morning.

When my beloved Terry passed away, I was beyond sad. I was crying, no I was sobbing. My brother was crying and my dad was trying not to show us that he was also attempting to hold back his tears. I stayed at the house for hours, prayed over my beautiful dog, and listened to my brother tell me how just before she died, she was calm. She walked into his room where he was sleeping and she gave him a slight courtesy bark and nudged him a bit so he would let her outside. He thought she just needed to go do her business outside. Instead she laid down in a sunny location next to our back sliding door and she went to sleep, for the very last time.

I still grieve, I still think of her, and I miss her so much. I often tell people this, I say, rather adamantly, that when I die and if I get to speak with God, (not that I believe God is a really powerful version of Gandalf The Grey, or something) I'm going to ask (Him/Her) what were you thinking when you created Dogs? You could have given them a much longer life span! What the heck was that all about, God? Big Mistake! I know you don't make mistakes, but boy if you did, that would sure be in the Top 5!

My dad was watching me pet Terry and cry my heart out. We were all so very sad. Terry lived a very long life for a dog. She had some adventures, and she was definitely loved and cared for. My dad watched us and then he left and walked back into the house. I left Terry with my brother, just to go check on my dad. I found him standing in the kitchen in front of the sink, looking out our kitchen window, and trying to fight back his tears. I walked over to hug him, because he was hurting, and I wanted to give him a consoling hug. He angrily grunted at me and pushed me away. I let that one hurt. I'm confused again.

When it was time to pick up my husband at the bus stop, I was still crying. I continued to cry while I cooked dinner for us, and while I cleaned up and washed the dishes. I kept on crying in bed while he was trying to sleep. I could not stop. I tried to stop my grieving, but I could not. I tried to silently weep. He kept telling me to stop it. He was getting angry. I was very pregnant, soon to give birth to our baby, and I had just experienced the passing of my best friend. Terry was literally my best friend. All he could think about was that I was keeping him awake. I stood up and tried to get him to understand how painful all of this was for me. I tried to show him how I felt, I said, "My dog, my very best friend; my sweet Terry died. How can you be so heartless?" He stood up, and for just a quick moment, I actually thought he was going to wrap his compassionate arms around me and say something loving and kind; you know, like he'd let me know that it's okay to grieve the loss of a beloved pet. But nope, as he stood up, he yelled, "Shut the Fuck Up!!" Then he punched me in the face. It was a right hook smack in my eye, and BAM! I hit the floor hard on my tummy. Yet another male had hit me, and this time I was 8 months pregnant.

He never made it to work the next morning, because he ended up having to take me to the ER. I had to walk into the Emergency Room, as a very pregnant *teenage woman*, (those two words sound very contradictory to me) and with a huge, swollen black eye. Very quickly my baby's heartbeat was listened to, and I was assured that my baby was fine. I had to stay away from my Dad until that shiner was completely gone. Even though my dad had done terrible, ugly things to hurt me, if he knew I was punched like that and while I was expecting a baby, he would have done some serious damage to him.

The next time I saw my father, it was after my beautiful, bouncing, baby boy was born. As far as I know, my father never knew what had happened. I made up my mind right then and there, I would leave my baby's father as soon as I could. Six months later that is exactly what I did.

What Are Your Takeaways?

After some deep, slow breaths, when you are ready, go ahead and ask yourself the following questions:

1. Did you continue to be abused by another person(s) after the childhood abuse had ended?
2. Are you able to see the patterns in your life Now as an Adult Survivor?
3. What can you do Now as an Adult, to break those patterns?

Chapter 11

LOOKING FOR LOVE IN ALL THE WRONG PLACES

Wɪᴛʜ ᴀ ʟɪᴛᴛʟᴇ ʙᴀʙʏ ɪɴ tow, I looked for work. I kept on trying to make ends meet. I was never able to secure child support from my baby's father. He was angry that I left him. He was also very selfish, and he had a drinking/substance abuse problem that I didn't pay much attention to back then, because it was only in the early stages of development. I was far too busy taking care of my newborn son.

His father was a full-blown alcoholic, who eventually drank himself to death. He fell and hit his head in a drunken stupor and he died. To be brutally honest, I did not miss the guy at all. He always gave me the creeps. I did not like him around my baby; not one bit. He was always drunk, and my baby's father never called him out on that fact. I took matters into my own hands, and I never let him hold my son. Once, he held my baby once, when he was about as close to being sober as he could ever get. It was when he drove over to our apartment to see his new grandson for the very first time.

I kept my baby a good distance away from him. It was not much longer after that when he fell and died. I found the whole thing quite sad.

I wanted to be loved. I had this beautiful little baby to love and care for, and I wanted him to have a "normal" childhood. I wanted him to have a Daddy. Not the daddy he had, but one who would be strong, confident, loving and kind. I spent a long part of my life looking for love in all the wrong places, falling in love with all the wrong men. It is true we attract what we reflect back to the Universe.

I struggled. I gave myself away far too easily. So many of us do this. We grow up abused, neglected and unloved and we give our bodies away as if they are the currency we exchange for what we ultimately seek – To Be Loved. Rarely does that work out for us. How can it, when we have not learned that we cannot receive the love we seek from another, until we have created a Love for our own selves.

I was always small and very petite, thin, never weighing more than 100 lbs. I never had any trouble attracting boys. That was always part of the problem, I was cute, and I was vivacious. I'm no wall flower. I was always a leader, never a follower. I guess some boys and men found that combination attractive. The only problem with that is, I was not well. I was looking for love in all the wrong places.

What Are Your Takeaways?

Take some Deep breaths, slowly, and breathe from your Diaphragm. When you are ready, and hopefully you are in your sacred space when you do this work... go ahead and,

Ask yourself the following questions:

1. Did you have any children at a young age?
2. Did you struggle with child-rearing because you were abused?
3. Did you look for love in all the wrong places?
4. How does the Adult you are now feel about the decisions you made back then?

Chapter 12

HARLEYS, HELLS ANGELS AND HOLLYWOOD

Somehow, for some reason, when I write this chapter, I hear the cool, sexy Texas drawl of Matthew McConaughay saying, in the way that only Matthew can, alright, alright, Alright!

Life for me as a single mother with absolutely no skills other than waitressing, cleaning toilets and changing diapers at 18 was difficult. No, it was extremely difficult. I had a friend, a boy, in elementary school. I'll call him Steve. He told himself that I was his girlfriend. I did not agree with him, but okay, we were still friends. Steve liked to hold my hand. This was not allowed in Elementary school, at least not back when I was a kid. We often walked home from school together. I wish Steve would have been there with me the day Leon lost his cool. Steve would have decked him. Maybe that's the real reason why Leon never touched me again. Steve probably told Leon, if you put one finger on her, ever again, it'll be the last thing you'll ever do! I would have liked that.

Steve and I remained friends for many years. We lost touch with each other after I was moved out of my home and in with my oldest sister and had to attend highschool in Granada Hills. After my son was born and after years of trying to earn enough money to keep a roof over our heads, food on the table and clothes on our backs, I practically begged my father to do something to get me an interview, and help me get a job at the General Motors, Van Nuys, Plant. For those of us who worked there, it was simply called, The Plant.

My father was not very pleased about my working there, he knew how many men were going to be trying to get into my pants. He had made it very clear over the years, why a man would have any interest in me. His exact words were, "Men will only want you for your Pussy." That's some excellent fatherly advice right there, Dad. Oh, well. Live and Learn. Live and Learn.

I did get that job working on the assembly line at the GM, Van Nuys Plant. What a wild ride that was. I am about 20 years old now, with a 2-year-old little boy. The money was good for me and my son and the work was hard. Every job on the assembly line can get bumped by seniority. If someone had more seniority than I did, they could file with their Union Representative and bump into my job on the line. There was this one woman who constantly did this to me. She'd just follow me around taking my job spots on the line. At one point I transferred to the day shift so I would be able to take my son to childcare and pick him up in the late afternoon, this allowed me to have a more normal work schedule. However, the only job that was available for me was in what was known as The Dungeon, because it was dark, dirty and dingy. This was where the first parts of what would eventually become a bright, shiny new car began. I joined the ranks of the Spot Welders. With sparks flying all around me, and my tiny frame, I tried desperately to hold my own with 99.9% of the men who worked with me in the Dungeon. What a trip that was.

After a few years of not seeing or hearing from Steve, well, what do you know? Guess who's working at the Plant with me? Yep, he's there. He's a few years older and a tad worse for wear. He's still my friend from our elementary school days though, only now he has purchased a house, has a wife and a new baby. I hang out with him on our lunch breaks. I worked the night shift, because I liked to drive to the beach in the mornings. While I never did learn how to surf using a surfboard, I'm most definitely a Southern California beach girl at heart. I went body-surfing all the time, and I did ride the cool waves with a Boogie Board. The beach is my happy place. There was a whole lot of drinking and pot smoking that went on during lunch breaks at that Plant.

Steve always wanted to be a biker. This was the 1970's and Biker's ruled, at least in Steve's mind they did. He had invited me over to his house to attend a party he was having on Saturday night. I would be able to meet his wife and see his new baby. I was in an on again, off again, relationship with my boyfriend, Jon, at the time, who also worked at the plant, but not on the assembly line. He was a Millwright. We had a fight which was quite often the case, because he was married, and although he told me, quite clearly, that he was going to be getting a divorce, he still had not done it.

He was thirteen years older than me, and I wasn't even the legal drinking age yet. Normally, when these fights would happen, I would stay home feeling sorry for myself, and wait for my phone to ring. Not this time. My young son was staying with my mom overnight. I decided I would go to Steve's party. What a night that turned out to be.

It wasn't enough for Steve to be a biker, i.e., by his being a bike owner. He already had a few of those. He actually desired, rather passionately, to live the life of a biker, as in, The Hells Angels, kind of bikers. It just so happens that the Hells Angels were in town on the day of Steve's party.

I take my son to my Mom's house, eat an early dinner with them and then say goodnight to my little boy. I have no clue about what's going to happen when I arrive at Steve's house. I had just purchased a brand new 1977 Pontiac Firebird. It was a beautiful car. White exterior with plush sky-blue interior seating. Remember, I was a Rock 'n' Roll kind of girl. Fast cars, loud music and always looking for someone to just love me for who I was and not what I had between my legs like my father always told me.

I get myself all fixed up, hair, check. Makeup, check. Cute outfit, check. My beautiful, white Firebird and I are off to Steve's party, and I'm hoping my boyfriend stops by my apartment unexpectedly, with a 6-pack of beer in hand, as he often did, to find that I'm not home waiting around on a Saturday night for him to come rushing back into my open arms. No. Not me. Not this time. I have options.

I get to Steve's and there are a lot of cars up and down the street, and bikes (think Choppers) parked on his driveway and in his garage. I go inside, Steve, with beer in hand as usual, is very happy I made it to his party and he can't wait to introduce me to his wife and their new baby. I always felt sorry for Steve's wife, she was quite young, we all were. I know all too well what it's like to be a young mother, married or single, with a baby to take care of. It is a lot of work. To have a husband who has not grown up yet and still holds on to his boyhood dream of being accepted as a

Hells Angel, does not make for a healthy marriage, let alone healthy parenting.

I met Steve's wife, who's name I have since forgotten. She seemed very nice, but not at all too happy that her husband is having this party. Who could blame her? She was probably up all night with the baby, changing diapers, breastfeeding her little one and trying to get some much needed sleep. Steve told her to go get their baby, and she's not at all happy with that order from him. She tries to explain to him that she just got the baby to sleep. Steve shows no signs of understanding what that takes, and insists she go get the baby and bring him out into the living room so I can see him. Very reluctantly, she does. Their baby was adorable, and he's still asleep in his mother's arms. I congratulate them both, and motion for her to go put her baby back in his bed, and to get some much needed sleep for herself.

We all hang out for about an hour or so at Steve's then he gets a phone call. There were no cell phones back then and all calls were either made or received on land lines. Steve is on his phone talking with a friend of his who lives in the next town over, he's quite excited. I have no idea why. He hangs up the phone, and announces to all of us that the party is being moved over to the guy's house who just called him. So, everyone gets up, gets in their cars or bikes and in an instant, Steve's wife had peace and quiet.

In less than 10 minutes we arrive at our destination. The garage is up, there are some very large, burly-looking dudes tinkering on some Harley's and guzzling down a six pack or two. The air is thick with the scent of Reefer. Outside on the front yard, which had patches of grass still struggling to grow, but was mostly dirt, there were Harley's everywhere. If you weren't riding a Harley, you just weren't cool.

Choppers, as we would call them, and Hogs. Many of these bikes were ridden by the visitors that Steve was so darned excited to meet. They had flown over from New Zealand. I had never met anybody from New Zealand before. Now, I was meeting the President of the New Zealand Chapter of the Hells Angels. Yes, those Hells Angels.

There are biker dudes all over the place and biker chicks. I'm not being derogatory here, that is what they called themselves, "biker chicks." I stayed close to Steve, because I did not know anybody there except for him. After a couple of hours, Steve decided we should go back to his place. I drove back to his house in my car, and a smaller group of the bikers followed.

Back at Steve's we all start getting to know one another. The president of the New Zealand Hell's Angels, I can clearly see, is quite interested in me. Although at this point even he doesn't know why. I'm cute, yes. I'm in excellent shape, yes, and I'm cool, yes. But what he finds out later as the evening progresses is that I'm smart. I am street smart, and I have my wits about me.

He asks me about my car. He really liked my new car. He wants me to take him out for a drive in it. It's a beautiful summer night, and I'm not drinking and I'm not at all high. He says he has always wanted to see Hollywood. He'd like to see Grauman's Chinese Theatre and walk the Hollywood Hall of Fame[4] on Hollywood Boulevard. It's still early in the evening, and so far, I'm enjoying our conversation. Although, I'm not at all sure I'm safe here with these Hells Angels. Especially the big guy, named Tiny. What is it with bikers, they always name the largest, most burlliest of dudes, Tiny?

Tiny was not the sharpest tool in the shed. He was definitely missing a lug nut, or maybe it was all the alcohol he was drinking. He was hanging out in the kitchen with a

---

[4] "Hollywood Walk of Fame - Wikipedia." https://en.wikipedia.org/wiki/Hollywood_Walk_of_Fame. Accessed 31 Jul. 2023.

couple of biker chicks. He muttered to them about how he might, as the night progressed and he got even more drunk; and even more stupid, decide to rape me and leave me for dead. Ha Ha Ha, they all laughed at how funny that was. Immediately, I looked up at him with the stare that only I can give. My sons have seen that look, that stare, that only a mother can give. Which basically translated to, try it mother fucker, and prepare to be shocked at what I will do. This is what I told myself I would do, so that Tiny would not succeed.

I would throw myself out that plate glass window and land in the backyard before that asshole could touch me. I openly admit this thinking of mine, as insane as it sounds, because I know you have probably put your own life on the line more than once, even if it was to avoid more pain. We become very adept fighters. We also tend to not think things through so well. This is what happens when you are used to staying in a Fight/Flight/Freeze state-of-mind all the time. It is both dangerous and it is exhausting.

In an instant, I had already decided what I would do to stop him. This, after all, was my pattern. It's what I knew. Tiny may have thought he would rape and kill me, but I would never allow that to happen. Even if it meant harming, maybe even killing, my own self in the process. Just like when my father was constantly hitting me on my head, and I told him, "That's nothing, Dad! I'll show you how you hit someone on the head, and I threw my head against the wall of that bedroom. You want to inflict pain, I'll show you what pain feels like." Yes, I know that anger and that rage, all too well. It was necessary to our survival.

I immediately left that kitchen and walked back over to Steve and the president guy, who's name I have also since forgotten. They really wanted to go to Hollywood, and since I had this beautiful brand new car, what a better way for us to go. I drove the president of the New Zealand chapter of the Hells Angels to Hollywood, California that hot, summer night. He sat shotgun, Steve and one other NZ Hells Angels dude sat next to Steve in the backseat. Off we went to tour Hollywood.

It was a beautiful night, Hollywood was bustling with tourists from around the world. Although, I'm pretty sure I'm the only one who brought a couple of New Zealand Hell's Angels to Hollywood that night. I parked the car, and out we went. This was back when Hollywood was still something to see. It's been downgraded over the decades, as far as I'm concerned.

California has been flooded with a huge homeless population over the decades since then, and it's a darn shame what is happening in this state. Freeways are mostly gridlocked, crime is at an all time high, and the cost of housing is through the roof. There has been a mass exodus of people leaving the state.

On that particular night there was no gridlock, and there was plenty of parking. We were not hounded by homeless people, sadly looking for a handout, nor were we accosted by criminals. Besides, who in their right mind would try and steal from these two guys? They were big, and they were strong and they were both from Hell. I actually felt quite safe. We all had a great time. They did some shopping for souvenirs, and we had dinner at one of the many Hollywood restaurants, who served Hells Angels. It was very fun to watch these two guys be surprised by the sights, sounds and tastes of Hollywood, California. We went to Grauman's Chinese Theatre[5], where they looked at all the

---

[5] "TCL Chinese Theatre: The Story of an L.A. Icon | Discover Los Angeles." 18 May. 2023, https://www.discoverlosangeles.com/things-to-do/tcl-chinese-theatre-the-story-of-an-la-icon. Accessed 23 Jun. 2023.

footprints of the famous Hollywood stars they had heard about and seen in movies.

Eventually, we had to go back to Steve's house. Steve had left his wife and baby there alone in the house with some of those partiers, including Tiny and the biker chicks. I'm sure she kept herself locked up in their bedroom all alone with her baby, absolutely fuming at what her husband had just put her through.

We got back to the house, and Tiny was still mouthing off. I was happy to go to Hollywood for no other reason but to get the Hell (pun intended!) away from Tiny. I sat on the sofa, and I picked the brain of the president. We talked for hours upon hours until it was daylight. I have always been quite inquisitive. I love to learn new things, gain new information and other perspectives about life, people, and the world in general. I found myself asking him, "Did you ever kill anyone?" He kind of laughed, as if to say, well, if I did, I wouldn't be able to tell you. I wanted to know what made him make that choice, to become a Hells Angel? Why would someone choose that sort of life? I have always been the "Who made liquid soap and why?" type of girl. I find all these fascinating things that make people tick. Why do people do the things that they do and why do they make the decisions, good, bad, or indifferent, that they make?

Now you might be thinking okay, this is the part where you two start making out on the sofa, right Marie? Or, you go into a back room and have Hell's Angel Biker and California Girl sex? Nope. None of that happened. He was actually quite the gentleman. Who would've thought, and a Hells Angel at that! Well, at least with me he was. We talked. That's all we did, and to this day, I wish I would have found a way to stay in touch with him, because he was really fun to talk with and he was very sweet. As they say, never judge a book by its cover. I'm sure many people would take one look at him, with his long, very long, blonde hair and his biker boots and chains, his Hells Angels patches all over his jacket, his scruffy facial hair and tattoos and make their judgements that this was a very dangerous, bad dude. I don't think he ever really harmed anyone. He never said he did. He just looked the part and he acted the part. Deep down, he was just looking for what every single one of us is looking for. To believe He was good enough, to be appreciated for who he was, and to be loved.

What Are Your Takeaways?

Now is the time, get quiet and centered. Breathing in slowly, and breathing out slowly, and being Calm in body/ mind. Ask yourself the following questions:

1. Did you settle for relationships with people who mistreated you?
2. Did you abstain from sexual activity, or did you become promiscuous as a subconscious way of getting back?
3. There are no right or wrong answers here. Write your feelings and beliefs about what your life was like after the childhood abuse stopped.
4. What were, if any, the acts of rebellion you displayed?
5. Why, as the Adult you are Now, do you believe you did those things?

Chapter 13
SHE'S A REBEL WITH A CAUSE

IN RETROSPECT, OUR FAMILY ENVIRONMENT was not normal in the least. Unless, of course, normal is the new dysfunctional. My parents were very shocked and distraught at my leaving home. Although, I don't know how they could not have seen the clues and the signs I was dropping all over the place before I actually did the dastardly deed.

I was at an age where fighting back was something I could actually do. My parents witnessed my anger, my fears and the volcanic explosion that was my rage. It is justified rage, so it's the best kind of rage there is. Their 16-year old teenage daughter was rebelling, big time. I threw fits of rage and turned 50 shades of scarlet every time I vented. I would scream back at him telling him how much I hated him, and I did, I hated him with a Vengeance that could not be quelled. I guess they had never really considered what the actual repercussions would be for turning a blind eye to the monster they had both created. The time for a rude awakening had begun.

He stood in the bedroom where he had perpetrated years of sexual abuse against me. He was angry over something I said. I believe this was when, for the first time, I called him a Bastard. He reacted by hitting me on top of my head, which was his usual M.O. This time, I had had enough! I yelled back at him, "You did not hit me hard enough, Dad! That didn't even hurt! Here, let me show you how to hit me on my head and make it really hurt!" I slammed the back of my head into the wall right beside him. The force of the impact reverberated throughout the room. He could not help but take notice of my behavior. It became clear that I had reached a breaking point, and that the mental anguish and trauma inflicted upon me had become unbearable.

Perhaps it was time for him to take responsibility for his actions and acknowledge the devastating impact they had on my young life. It was clear that I was no longer willing to suffer in silence, nor should I be expected to. My mother was in the kitchen again, listening to us fight. I continued to scream "It's time to seek professional help for your "Mother Fucking mental disease!", as I so boldly put it. It was crucial that both my father and my mother step-up and begin to support me on my journey (and theirs) towards healing and recovery. The consequences of failing to do so could be dire.

Thank God, we did not have PC's back then and the horrors that can often be created using social media, run amuck. I probably wouldn't be writing this book right now, and you would not be reading it. It's quite possible that if I did, instead of sharing my deepest pains and fears with my friend, I may have reached out to the world for advice, and these days, that's a surefire way to get pushed – even dared – into committing suicide. Technology is great until it isn't, I always say. My opinion is that taking your own life is never the answer. I consider it the easiest way out. I always chose to stay and slay my own demons. They have no real power over me, I decide what my Identity will be, this is my life and it is my Destiny I AM Creating.

What appeared to people on the outside as my being a very spoiled, little brat, who had her own pony, you know, the "spoiled" baby of the family, was not quite as it seemed. Often, the youngest in the family is very vulnerable because older siblings have moved out on their own, or are far too busy with college, university, work and living their own lives to be bothered with their younger sibling's tantrums. However, sometimes tantrums are a cry for help.

Was I assertive, absolutely! Was I aggressive? No doubt about it and I was proud of that fact! I was a fighter just like my Dad was. In our household, we were made to, almost on a daily basis, listen to our Father's stories about the Germans and Hitler and WWII. Whether we wanted to hear my dad's stories or not, it did not matter. After many, decades of hearing the same stories, all of us, including our mother, could practically finish his stories for him. It seemed as if everytime I turned around, my father was bringing up WWII.

When I think about my father and his incessant war stories, I always relate to one of the love's of my life, a man I have adored for a very, very long time, Jackson Browne. Jackson's songs have always touched my heart and soul deeply. Not to mention the fact that Jackson Browne was drop-dead gorgeous with his chiseled chin, large, dreamy brown eyes and that hair! Not too long, not too short, those deep, brown locks just swayed to his music like all us girls did! Oh, boy, do I ever digress! In *The Pretender*, a brilliant anthem of Jackson's he poetically writes and sings about the *Veteran, who dreams of the fight, fast asleep at the traffic light.* Yes, Jackson, you just described my dad to a T as in PTSD. Thank you for helping me to not feel so all alone.

I liked listening to my dad's WWII stories. I was proud

of him. I was proud of his war medals. There were family films and photographs of me holding his medals in which I'm beaming with pride that this man, this war hero, is my Dad. I know there was a film of me at around 6 years-old, holding his Purple Heart medal. I didn't quite understand what it all really meant. How can a child grasp a concept as gigantic as a World War? All I knew was that my Dad was a hero. He fought against the evil German soldiers. He helped to save the entire world from the evils of a Nazi murdering nut! He fought alongside our British allies, and he helped America, England, and our loyal allies, win the war against Japan, Germany, Italy and put an end to WWII. Even as a very young child of only about 7 years old, I was proud my Dad was a war hero in something that I knew only from watching WWII movies with him. In battle, he was hit by Bazooka shrapnel and survived, while so many others gave their very lives. He could talk about his wartime stories all he wanted. I hung on to his every word. He was my Hero. That is, until I grew up.

After all the good times, the not so good times, and the happy moments along with the gut-wrenchingly painful years of my life, I AM ALIVE! I Survived it all. Unless you have been rock bottom at some point in your life, and unless you have suffered through a very dark night of the soul, and came out of it scathed, but still able to give and receive LOVE, you may not yet fully understand just how Powerful those words I just stated, truly are. There will always be people who have seemingly better lives than you, just as there will always be people who seem to have worse life's circumstances than you.

What are the main issues causing you concern? Is it the constant traffic jams? Are you dealing with a difficult boss at work? Have you discovered that your spouse has been unfaithful? Perhaps you've recently misplaced your wallet? Are you feeling unsure about your life's goals? Are you unhappy with your current job? Is your marriage on the rocks as your spouse expresses their desire for a divorce? Have you recently suffered a broken leg or gotten into a car accident resulting in significant damage to your beloved vehicle? Does it seem like each day at 5:00 PM, you're plagued by a pounding headache?

My mother did not kick her husband to the curb. She certainly did not call the police and have him arrested. She was not strong enough for any of that. She made her abused, frightened, angry, extremely messed up and very confused young teenage daughter leave her home. I adored and needed my Mother. Their answer to this problem was to take the teenager out of her bedroom, which was my only safe place, until I was being groomed and then sexually abused. I loved my dog. I grew up with that dog. My dog, our family dog, did not do a damn thing wrong. The one person who was always with her, who fed her, picked up her dog poop, gave her belly rubs, played with her, taught her tricks, and loved her, completely and unconditionally, was me. I'm forced to leave her behind. Yeah, that makes about as much sense as kicking me out of the house.

You want to create drama? Then take a young teenage girl who's already been abused by her own Biological Father, and ship her off to her sweet, passive, loving and kind older sister. I had to change highschools. Yes, that's a recipe for disaster. Add in some California Beach Girl & Hippie vibes, Rock 'n' Roll, Led Zeppelin, then sprinkle in some David Bowie and Alice Cooper and you have the makings of a Wild Child. Free at last, free at last, thank God, I was free at last! Or, so I thought.

Now, I'm out of the house, the only home I had ever known. I have left my mother, my Dog, my friends, my neighbors, my community, and my high school. Many of my friends in high school were friends I had gone to junior high school with. Some of them I had known since my elementary school days. My best friend was one of them. Remember, she's the one who talked me into running away.

Who knows what could have happened if she didn't. It could have become very ugly, that's for sure. We were teenagers. What did we know about life? About being smart? About being safe and how I would feel when running away from home. She believed he had to be stopped. The only way to do that was to get me away from him. We saw running away from home as my only viable option. Calling the police was not a viable option for me. Back then, nobody talked about calling the police for help over something as personal as sexual child abuse. In many families, it is still kept a deep, dark, family secret.

It may have been an option to get him to stop harming me, but then I had to think about what it would do to my mother and my siblings. It felt as if the entire weight of the world was placed upon my shoulders. My concern was how do I protect myself and not hurt anyone I love in the process. This is not a decision a 16 year old girl should be forced to make. Unfortunately, based on results, it happens all the time.

During the runaway timeframe, which added up to about 2 months. I'm taken to one location first, but I could not stay there because it was too obvious that I would be easily caught. My parents knew where their house was. So, it was decided to quickly take me to the 2-bedroom apartment of my friend's oldest sister's friend. It's the early 70's and smoking pot was huge, just like it was in the 60's and I guess not much has changed over the decades, because now in California, where I'm from, Marijuana is legal. I'm brought into this apartment and my friend stayed with me for a while which made me feel more comfortable. Although, eventually, she has to leave and go back to school. I'm not going back to school, because I ran away from home. It's all so crystal clear in my memory, but without the pain. I can see it all in my mind's eye, exactly as it happened.

I no longer suffer through the nightmares, and I'm no longer triggered, like I used to be. I have been over the sadness, grief and the suffering of it all for many years now. I see the blessings from these experiences. They have given me strength, survival skills, and the ability to make something of my life even with the insurmountable odds against my survival. Then again, odds do not have anything to do with it, do they? When I was knocked down I always picked myself up, dusted myself off and put one foot courageously in front of the other and powered through to the next chapter of my life. I learned those Life Lessons, and I was the better for it. I carried on. You Can too! Yes, you Can.

I eventually self-admitted myself to a psychiatric in-house clinic for people suffering with alcoholism, and/or drug addiction. I did not have either of those ailments, but I was depressed, and I was confused, very, very confused. All I wanted was to be a good mother, and to be happy.

I was overwhelmed with feeling not good enough, and nobody in my immediate family could help me. My father would have continued to abuse me, if he only could, while he continued to tell me how much he loved me. My childhood, if not obviously frightening, painful and horrific, was in one word: CONFUSING.

I wanted to know who I was, why I was here and what it was that I was meant to do. My mother was in complete denial. My older sister tried, but he scared her away. My oldest brother did not know any of this was happening. He did not live at home any longer. My other sister just didn't give a damn. As long as our father was not sexually abusing her, she was happy for it to be happening to me. I always looked up to her when I was a kid. I thought she was smart and cool. I could not understand why she didn't seem to like me very much back then. Maybe this is what she needed to do to justify it to herself so that she did not have to care. She did not reach out and attempt to do anything to help me. Decades later, and after our Mother had passed, she called me on the phone and apologized for wanting me to be the one who was abused by our father and not her. My sister did the best she could with who she was at that time. I heard her and I understood her, and all is forgiven.

I remember one day during a group session with two of the counselors who were leading a group 'share' session, and when it came time for me to say how I felt out loud, to the group, I said the following:

"I don't like people. I hate people. All people do is hurt you. I only love dogs. Dogs love unconditionally. Dogs will never hurt me. I don't like people, and I don't need people. I only need Dogs."

I said those words and I meant every word I uttered. This was not simply a 21-year old woman venting. I had learned that people cause me pain. I did not want to risk being hurt by a human being ever again. My mother came to this session. She shrugged her shoulders after hearing me say those words. She looked at the two very young men leading the group as if to say…what do I do with her?

One of the guys laughed and said, "Oh, you don't mean that." Well, in reality, I did mean it. I can't help but think if Tony Robbins[6] was leading that group and I uttered those words, I highly doubt he would have left it like that. I'm sure

---

[6] "Mission | Robbins Madanes Training." https://rmtcenter.com/mission/. Accessed 20 Jul. 2023.

he would have done a Strategic Intervention[7] right there on the spot, and I would have been understood. Instead, I got these two egotistical know-it-alls laughing at me in front of the entire group and in front of my mother while I'm being vulnerable and bearing my soul; so naturally, yes, my life continued to spiral out of control.

Jon asked me to go with him to live in Las Vegas, Nevada. He had spoken with a friend of his who could hire him as a Millwright. He said it would be better for us if we left California, because his soon-to-be ex would not be harassing him all the time. I, of course, said I would go with him, and my young son would go with me. My mother was very concerned about us leaving.

Before we left the house for Las Vegas, my mother had asked Jon to promise her he would not leave us abandoned and all alone in Las Vegas. She told him that if he felt he would leave again, to please call her and let her know. She knew I would be stuck there with her precious young Grandson without a car to drive us back home to California. She also knew I would most likely have very little money. It turned out that my mother was right.

[7] "Using Strategic Intervention - What Is Strategic Intervention?." 10 Oct. 2018, https://strategicintervention.info/strategic-intervention/. Accessed 24 Jul. 2023.

What Are Your Takeaways?

Allow yourself to be calm, relaxed and take some long, slow, deep breaths and ask yourself the following questions:

1. Did you get any help, support and understanding as a child? If so, from whom and what were your results?
2. Did you go into therapy, and if so what happened? Were you happier as a result?
3. What were the beliefs you told yourself as you struggled to survive your past?
4. What are your beliefs Now, as an Adult?
5. Are you stronger Now? If so, How?

Chapter 14
LEAVING LAS VEGAS

I HUGGED MY MOTHER GOOD-BYE AND she hugged and kissed her sweet Grandson goodbye, and we drove to Las Vegas, NV. Once we arrived and settled in, I went to a job interview at a casino. It was off the strip, and across from a large truck stop. I was hired on the spot. I actually had a lot of fun working there. The red and black, Saloon Girl uniform, complete with black choker was very pretty. I worked behind the bar, and also served drinks to those who were gambling. Most of the truckers stopped in for a beer or two or three… I had a fantastic time getting to know them. The tips were good. It was the Old West Saloon, where everybody knows your name.

I enrolled my young son, now a Kindergartner, at an elementary school close to the house we were staying at. The house was owned by Jon's friend. Things were going well, I thought. Jon and I were both working. We both had steady incomes. My son enjoyed his Kindergarten class. He was making friends. I did not have to be concerned about his dad drinking when he came over to visit his son, because we were out of state, and he rarely came over to visit his son even when we lived in California. My son and I loved to watch the thunderstorms in Las Vegas. Ever since I was a child I have always loved lightning and thunder. The Nevada Light Show that Mother Nature puts on in that state is nothing short of amazing, but I digress.

We seemed to be doing okay. Other than the fact that we had no furniture, Jon and I slept on the floor on blankets. My son slept on a twin mattress set and he had his own room. He had plenty of toys to play with, and he liked going to school. The plan was to save up enough money to get our own home. That never happened. About 6 months later, I had a surprise.

I'm pregnant. Jon is the father and he has been told. I actually believed he would be happy about the news. He tried to be, to not upset me. He had so many addiction issues back then. Las Vegas is not very conducive to helping one live a Clean and Sober life. There is temptation on every corner. Sure enough, he does exactly what my mother asked him not to do, within a few days, he is gone. He had done this before. Back in California, one day he'd be renting an apartment, and then several months later he completely vanished. I was so desperate for love, and for this relationship to not fail, that I would go out looking for him. We do things when we are not whole. When our wounds own us instead of us owing our wounds, people get hurt, including ourselves. People get fractured when their sense of self-worth and self-love are destroyed.

When Jon did not come home from work that night, I intuitively knew something was not right. I told myself to stay calm, I did not want anyone, especially my little boy, to know anything was wrong. Maybe Jon was out at the casinos gambling away his paycheck? Lord knows he had done that before. I thought about all the excuses I made so I did not have to look at the truth. We know the ugly truth about what's really happening with our relationships, but often we don't want to face them because it will be far too painful. Thoughts like, maybe he stopped somewhere to have a beer with a friend, maybe he's working OT and he can't get to a phone, maybe he had an accident and he's in the hospital, and they don't know I'm his girlfriend, and they're contacting his soon to be ex-wife, or maybe he's at a stripclub, they sure have an ample supply of those in Las Vegas, maybe he's having sex with someone else, Right Now!

I walked outside in the backyard. It grew dark outside, as I looked up at the brilliant twinkling of stars in the Nevada night sky, I saw a flash of light sweeping over my head. It was a shooting star. I took that star to be an omen. To me it meant, everything is going to be alright. Everything works out as it's supposed to. I went back into the house and I looked at the dinner I had prepared for him. It was as cold as ice, just like he was. I stopped telling myself all the possible excuses, and faced the painful, obvious truth. He had done it again. I had been through this before, although not when I was pregnant. It really wasn't quite as painful as I thought it would be.

Maybe, it was because I knew I was not completely alone. His friend was there and his friend's girlfriend who had moved in with him. Most importantly, because my little boy was playing in the next room, on his mattress on the floor with his toys. Jon had lied to my mother that day, and more than anything, I was furious with him for lying to my mom. She did not deserve that. Before we left for Las Vegas, she asked him for one thing and one thing only, to promise her that he would not leave me all alone in Las Vegas. He promised her he would not leave me stranded alone again with my son.

He assured her, or so he thought he assured her. She did not believe any of his lies, or was taken in by his false charms. She knew he would do it again. That's what he did. He would behave like a coward when he didn't want to hurt someone, or have a fight. I'm sure in his mind he was doing the right thing. Better to just disappear and not get into a physical altercation with an emotional, and pregnant, soon to be ex-girlfriend. Especially with her child right there. Besides, what would his friends think? So, he just left. He left me no money for food, or plane tickets back home to California, not even a note explaining why. He never left notes, for someone who always had a lot to say, it's rather peculiar whenever he left, he never left a note.

After getting my son to sleep for the night. I walked back into our room and I cried it out, quietly. In the morning I got up and figured out what I was going to do. Jon's friend said we were welcome to stay there with him and his girlfriend. I did not think that was the best thing I could do for my boy. I needed to get him back home to California. He needed to be with his family who loved him. My family may have been dysfunctional, but we loved each other through thick and thin.

I called my mother and let her know what happened. She was not all that surprised, either. She expected that something like this would probably happen. I told her I was pregnant, and that's why he left so suddenly. She said she and my father would make the trip to Las Vegas to pick us up and take us back home to the house. Mom's home cooking sounded mighty fine to me. My son would be back in familiar territory and he would be with his loving grandparents. Yes, it meant I would have to stay at my parents house, the house where I was abused for years, but I was an adult now, I was pregnant, and I was keeping my baby. It was temporary anyway. It would be difficult, it would trigger all sorts of memories for me. It was the best and safest place for my young son at the time.

The thought of having an abusive father be present around one's own child may come across as surprising, or even alarming, to some individuals. However, in my personal experience, the matter was far from simple. It was evident that my father had a particular compulsion, a perverted craving that consumed him like a disease, to satisfy his lustful desires with his own daughters. He displayed no interest whatsoever towards my sons, who were his biological grandsons – none whatsoever.

It was clear that his preference lay solely with young females, particularly those who were related to him by blood. The complexity of this situation cannot be overstated. As a survivor of abuse, it was difficult for me to reconcile the fact that my abuser was still in my life, let alone in the life of my child. The fear and anxiety that I experienced were overwhelming, and I was constantly vigilant about keeping my son safe. It was a delicate balancing act, trying to maintain a semblance of normalcy while also remaining vigilant and protective.

Looking back on this situation, it is clear to me that the effects of abuse extend far beyond the initial acts of violence or exploitation. They infiltrate every aspect of the survivor's life, often with lasting consequences. In my case, the presence of my abuser in my life made it challenging to establish healthy boundaries and build trusting relationships. However, through therapy and other forms of support, I have been able to work through these challenges and build a fulfilling life for myself and my family.

My mother had insisted that I not say a word about my pregnancy to my father. My son sat in the front passenger seat as my Dad was driving. My mother and I sat in the back seats. We hadn't been on the freeway very long when we witnessed a terrible sight. There was a tall building on fire. It was to our left, as we were heading South on the 15 Freeway back towards Southern California. I can still see that scene in my mind's eye, as if it were yesterday. There were flames shooting out the windows, and black smoke billowing in the Las Vegas sky. It looked very bad. Traffic was slowed on the freeway, because so many people driving by slowed down to look at what was happening. Through the smoke and the flames we could see the name of the building. This was the day that the Las Vegas, Nevada, MGM Grand Hotel & Casino had caught on fire.[8]

We watched from our car and my Mother and I silently said prayers. My little boy had big dreams of one day becoming a Fireman. I had taken him to our local Fire Station's Open House since he was 2 years old. I grew up in a corner house watching car accidents, fires and all sorts of scary things happen right in front of my young eyes as a child, so taking my little boy to our local Fire House to let him sit in the fire engine at his first Fire Station Open House was so much fun for him. He had a great time, and right then and there he knew what his career path would be from that very first time he sat in that big, red, fire engine.

Now I watched my son watching the MGM burn, and his eyes were wide open. A mother knows what her children's callings are. If she's tuned-in to them, and paying close enough attention. I was. I had always known my #1 Son would become what he always said he would be, a Fireman.

42 years ago, that fire killed 87 people and injured more

---

[8] "42 years ago: Fire at MGM Grand Hotel killed 87 people, injured ...." 21 Nov. 2022, https://www.ktnv.com/news/42-years-ago-fire-at-the-mgm-grand-hotel-killed-87-injuring-more-than-600. Accessed 6 Jun. 2023.

than 600.[9] It also cemented in my child's heart and Soul, the belief that he would one day grow up and become who he was born to be. And that's exactly what he set out to do. He succeeded, far beyond my dreams for him. He became a Firefighter.

Earlier this year, he traveled to Turkey as part of US Task Force efforts in Search and Rescue looking for survivors after the devastating earthquakes.[10] I had no doubt while watching my young son with his eyes fixated on that tragic event unfolding in real time, that he would grow up to be one of the good guys. Little did I know, at that time, the baby growing inside my womb, as we all watched the devastating fire that morning; that spark of Divine Light, must have been watching too. He would also follow in his big brother's footsteps. Just 7 months later, my beautiful son was born. He, too, had the calling. Both of my son's are now serving as Fire Captains. This was, and has always been, their calling.

In the fall of 1994, my 3rd, and final, beautiful son made his grand entrance into the world. As he grew up I couldn't help but feel relieved that he did not choose to follow in his older brothers' footsteps and become a Paramedic/Firefighter. The thought of having my 3rd child putting himself in such danger was almost too much for my heart to bear. As it turned out, my son had a different calling altogether. From a very young age, it was clear to me that he possessed a creative genius that set him apart. Whether

[9] "42 Years Ago: The MGM Fire of 1980 and the Air Force Response ...." 21 Nov. 2022, https://www.nellis.af.mil/News/Article-Display/Article/3225337/42-years-ago-the-mgm-fire-of-1980-and-the-air-force-response/. Accessed 6 Jun. 2023.

[10] "Syria/Turkey Earthquakes Situation Report #7, March 8, 2023." 8 Mar. 2023, https://reliefweb.int/report/syrian-arab-republic/syriaturkey-earthquakes-situation-report-7-march-8-2023. Accessed 6 Jun. 2023.

it was his love of music, or writing and creating, he had a natural talent that always seemed to leave me in awe. As a parent, I consider myself incredibly blessed to have not just 1, but 3 amazing sons who are each gifts to this world. Each of them has their own unique strengths and talents, and I'm proud to be their loving Mother. Each of them, in their own special way, fills my heart with Joy and Laughter. I can honestly say that I love them with every fiber of my being, with all my Heart and Soul. No matter where they are, and no matter how busy they may be, I AM Always Connected to them in body/mind and Soul.

What Are Your Takeaways?

That was another tough chapter to write. I write and then I rest. I hope you too, are reading, writing in your Journal and then giving yourself a much needed rest to just be alone for awhile, and allow yourself to heal. Before your much deserved rest though, Now is the time to ask yourself the following questions:

1. Did you have any children? Write about your experiences.
2. Depending on your age now, do you have any grandchildren? What is it like for you being a grandparent?
3. How have you treated your own children (if any) and grandchildren differently than you were treated as a child?
4. What does parenting a child or children mean to you Now as an Adult?

Think about how often you hear that 'still, small voice' in your head. Who is speaking?

Chapter 15

WHY DID GOD ALLOW THIS TO HAPPEN?

$\mathcal{M}$Y PERSONAL BELIEFS ABOUT GOD in no way need to be yours. These are my beliefs, based on my own personal experience:

- God Does Not Intervene With Our Growth

  God is NOT some old man with long white hair and a beard, living up in the clouds, sitting on his golden throne, and looking down watching you through the clouds and making sure that you learn your lessons. God is not deciding whether or not HE/ SHE needs to punish you like a really mean version of Santa Claus.

- We choose to incarnate at a particular time, in a particular circumstance, in a particular country. This is my belief. This is what I have come to believe and know as my Truth, and while paying attention to the signs all around me. Again, I'm not saying these have to be your beliefs. Just allow yourself to be open to my words.

- Think of this World as a very big school for Soul Growth. A DIVINE SCHOOL. As Human Beings, we don't get to remember why we came here; as babies I believe we do remember. Babies can't communicate their memories. I believe that as we age, the further away our memories fade. This runs almost parallel to the development of a human being's attachment to the Egoic Mind.

- Yes. God Loves You. This is my personal belief. My experience of God is not a He or a She, God is Divine Intelligence. All That Is. God is Omnipresent, and Omnipotent. I usually say God, The Universe and often I speak of God as Divine Intelligence.

I constantly struggled with feeling bad, dirty, full of shame and guilt. It was made very clear to me that God did not love me anymore. Otherwise, why would He allow this to happen to me? When we carry this belief about ourselves, it is easy to see why we are not able to have love for our own selves. If God doesn't love us, how are we supposed to love ourselves?

What Are Your Takeaways?

Take some time Now in your sacred space, and write in your journal.

Ask yourself the following questions:

1. Is there anything you need to say to God? Is there anything you want to say to your Creator?
2. Do you believe in Jesus Christ? If you answered yes, what do you want to say to Jesus?
3. What did you believe about God back when the abuse first started? You may have been too young to have had any beliefs back then. If so, as you matured, what did you believe about God?
4. What are your beliefs about God, your Creator, now as an Adult?

Chapter 16
THE MUSTARD SEED

ONCE WHEN I WAS ABOUT 8 years old, I cherished a prized possession that held immense value to me. I wore it daily. It was an exquisite, crimson-colored necklace crafted with meticulous care, adorned with a slender cord. This inexpensive piece of jewelry captivated the attention of all who looked at it. At the end of the necklace a bottle was carefully secured and sealed shut. There was a single mustard seed within it. This seemingly insignificant mustard seed served a profound purpose in my life, acting as a constant, albeit, a gentle reminder of the invaluable teachings of Jesus Christ. It symbolized the power of unwavering faith, illustrating how even the tiniest mustard seed of belief could yield remarkable outcomes in one's journey through life. Through this humble seed, I learned a timeless lesson about unwavering faith and the transformative power it holds. The Kingdom of Heaven truly IS Within You.

Jesus Christ taught us all that With Faith, even as small as the size of a mustard seed, we can move mountains. Jesus taught that to have faith in who and what you are, you can co-create with God, aka, Divine Intelligence, (if you prefer) and know the Kingdom of Heaven is Truly Within You.

> So Jesus said to them, "Because of your
> unbelief; for assuredly, I say to you, if you have
> faith as a mustard seed, you will say to this
> mountain, 'Move from here to there,' and it will
> move; and nothing will be impossible for you.

Verse 17:20

Just like the mustard plant grows from such a tiny seed, so does even the tiniest seed of faith have the potential to blossom into great achievements and wonders, surpassing the limitations imposed by mere appearances. For me, this tiny seed encapsulated the essence of the Kingdom of Heaven itself. It taught me that true greatness and fulfillment are not in the grandeur or magnitude of our actions, but rather in the depth of our faith and the unyielding commitment to it. As I held this mustard seed in the palm of my hand, I could feel the weight of its significance and the boundless potential it represented. Every single time I glanced upon this unassuming seed, I was reminded of the immense power and presence of faith in my life: a force capable of moving mountains, making miracles possible, and guiding me through the darkest of times.

The mustard seed became a beacon of hope, an emblem of resilience, and a testament to the eternal truth that it is precisely when our challenges seem insurmountable that we must hold onto faith most tightly. Thus, this seemingly insignificant mustard seed transcended its physical form and evolved into a profound symbol in my existence. It instilled in me a sense of the miraculous and filled my heart with the unwavering belief that even the smallest, most overlooked aspects of life can hold immeasurable significance. As I walked through the journey of my own life, this mustard seed paved the way for a deep understanding that the Kingdom of Heaven lies not only in some distant realm but also within the depths of our souls, waiting to be discovered through the power of faith and love.

What Are Your Takeaways?

Time to get introspective. Breathe, slowly, and deeply. Get centered and ask yourself the following questions:

1. Did you have a religious upbringing as a child? If so, what was it?
2. What members of your family went to church, or other places of worship?
3. What beliefs did you form about yourself with regards to your religion as a child?
4. Do you practice a particular religion now as an adult?
5. How has that religion helped you as a childhood/ domestic abuse survivor?
6. Do you give thanks for all the Good that is in your life, now?
7. Where is your Faith now as an Adult?

"Let Yourself Be Whole Again"

~Jesus Christ

Chapter 17
WHY DO WE SUFFER?

*W*HY DO WE SUFFER? LONG after the abuse has stopped, we still suffer. Why do we do that? One of the reasons is because we still want justice. We need, we so desperately yearn for, the acknowledgement of our abuse from those we believe should be giving it to us. This can be from the abuser(s) themselves, or perhaps a family member(s) that we have told our experiences of abuse to. This is why we suffer so much and for so long. Some of us for decades. We can become attached to our past trauma by our need to have it all validated by these people. These people who may never be able to give you what you seek and desire so desperately. We think if:_____ (i.e., fill in the blank) would say he/she/they are sorry. If he/she/they would just see the pain I'm in and apologize to me for what he/she/they did, I could get on with my life. We rarely get the results we seek. Stop doing this to yourself.

It works out far better for you, especially in the long run, to let go of your attachment to these types of expectations.

Let go, or at the very least, set aside, your need to have your pain validated by people who may never be able to apologize for what they did to you. Let go of your need to have a family member acknowledge the terrible things that happened to you. They may never be capable of giving you what you desire and the longer you wait until they do, the longer you will experience pain. I'm talking about the pain that is emotionally, and physically going to continue to stew within your BodyMind, most likely which will eventually cause health issues. Stop trying so hard to get the results you desire from other people. The only results you need are the ones you create for yourself.

Let your expectations go. If the people you seek recognition from ever heal from what haunts them, and if they grow and evolve enough to eventually have a true awakening, which translates to: they become free from the bonds of Ego. Then they will come to you. Otherwise, stop chasing them for the results you believe you must receive in order to be happy. Never look to them for results. To do so gives them all your power.

You take your power back, by letting go of your need to be justified by all your pain and heartache. You want the anger you feel to be acknowledged by the very people who hurt you or from those who don't know how to help you. Don't do that to yourself. That's like trying to get blood out of the proverbial Turnip! Chances are it will be a cold day in Hell before that ever happens for you.

Stop expecting these people to be able to think right. To understand where they went wrong. To somehow grow themselves a massive amount of Compassion and Empathy. They may know, perhaps deep inside, that they wronged you. However, they may never, as long as they live, be able to apologize to you. They may never be able to give you love in the way you deserve, want and need so you give it to yourself.

What do you do with this knowledge? You do your very best to let them go. You are not condoning their actions. You are taking your Power Back! You are allowing yourself to heal. You are staying in the present moment and taking responsibility for your own future, instead of giving the power to other people. Stop giving them that power. Stop allowing your Egoic Mind to loop the memories you hold onto of that childhood abuse, because it continues to control your life. The past is over. You are here now. You take control of your life! Take Your Personal Power Back! This is the way to become Whole again.

What Are Your Takeaways?

Remember, as I share my story with you, allow yourself to think back to all the things you did in order to survive. He, She or They are no longer able to hurt you. Write about what you did in order to survive. What decisions did you make? What did you tell yourself about why it was happening?

Take some time, in your sacred space, whatever that may be for you and write in your journal. Our stories were very different and our abusers were different people, the circumstances we found ourselves in were different; and even though all that is true, we are very much the same in terms of what those experiences caused us to believe about ourselves and how those experiences made us feel.

Ask yourself the following questions:

1. Did you fill in the blank? If not, ask yourself, who do you want an apology from? Even more important, why do you think you need that apology?

    If only _____ would apologize to me.

2. If this person(s) apologized how would it help you to heal?

3. Do you realize that none of what they did to you really had anything to do with you? You were, simply put, available to him/her/them at that time.

4. Complete this sentence, I was only a child and none of it was my fault. I know this now, but when I was young I believed...

5. Complete this sentence, Now that I'm an adult, I know that it was never my fault. I did absolutely nothing wrong, and I now believe...

Chapter 18

LEVELING UP AND GROWING UP

ONE OF THE MOST DIFFICULT lessons survivors of childhood abuse struggle with accepting, and I'm speaking about those people who never had therapy, who never had help and support in learning how to overcome and transform the traumatic events in their lives, is the lesson of growing ourselves up. We tend to always be ready for the fight. We voraciously defend our right to be angry. Who would blame us? If people are made aware of the horrors we have suffered, we can receive a whole lot of sympathy and some much needed understanding. There's nothing wrong with that at all, and the fact is, that it is necessary and conducive to our survival. We need to be heard, we need to be understood and we need support, lots of support and love.

However, we must watch ourselves. We must be careful to not take advantage of people's compassion and never use it to entitle ourselves to continually play the Rage Card. Never allow your anger and rage to overpower you. There is a healthy dose of empowerment in anger, yes, but to a degree. You know when you are overstepping your bounds. You know when you are using your rage to control others. Even if you have never truly admitted it to yourself. Yes, it is an extremely difficult thing to do, but it is all part of the process of growing ourselves up, because we did not get the opportunity to be grown up; raised up, by at least one or in some cases, both of our parents. The good-parenting ball was dropped, and it is up to each of us to take that ball back and move it into our own court.

Sure others have caused us harm, but that does not mean we get to harm others. We are no longer children. We are grown adults, and it is for our highest good, and the highest good of others, and the world in general; for that matter, that we stop feeling sorry for ourselves and grow the hell up. I know that probably angers you to read, but it needs to be said. You were not taught how to be a mature adult, and you were severely traumatized at a very young age. So was I. In essence, we all had to work diligently on growing ourselves up. If you haven't yet looked at your anger, then there is no time like the present.

This doesn't mean you can't keep your inner child close to you, no, not at all. It is a true gift when we are able to tune into our childlike qualities. Allow yourself to laugh at funny jokes, be eager at blowing all the candles out on your birthday cake, and go ahead and throw abandon to the wind. Just refrain from stomping all over people in line at the check-out counter, or on the freeway that is now gridlocked, and never lash out at your own children or grandchildren because you were never taught to control your rage. We don't get to do that. If you are still doing that, please seek therapy or hire a Life Coach, especially one who has real life experience in overcoming childhood trauma and has transformed their own life. Take control of your temper, so your temper does not control you. Your life and the lives of those you love will be much happier when you do.

So many women ask me, and often struggle with the issue of Forgiveness. It is a very necessary topic to talk about right here and right now. Remember the choice to "forgive" or to "not forgive," is a personal choice. That choice is Always up to you. Nobody, not your mother, father, sister, brother, or other family members should be berating you to Forgive. They did not go through the experiences you suffered through. They have no business telling you what you should or should not do. It may be, however, that they are saying these things to you out of love. Is it possible they don't want to see you suffer anymore? Could that be true? Can you allow yourself to simply entertain that thought?

I will never suggest to you what you should or should not do when it comes to forgiveness. I can only speak to you from my personal experience. The abuse I suffered is in many ways going to be similar to yours, in terms of how it made you and I feel. Yet, at the same time, our experiences were very different. Only you can decide what is best for you. If you are currently in therapy, not even your therapist should be telling you that you must forgive; and I highly doubt a good therapist would. This is your choice and nobody else gets to make this decision for you.

The ability to forgive and the decision to forgive others who harmed you, comes from within you. If your intuition, your gut feeling, is that you want to forgive, then go ahead and forgive. You do not have to see this person, or people, again. It might be they are no longer alive, maybe there's a restraining order on them, maybe you have no idea where they are any longer. It's all ok. You can still forgive. The act of forgiveness is not really about them anyway. It's for you. In a way, it's as if you are cutting the ties that you have with them. It's a way of taking back your power. You only have so much Life Force Energy. If you are stuck in your past, if you are living now with any of your thoughts still battling someone for control, and to be right, for argument's sake, then you are wasting your precious Life Force Energy. I know this based on my own experience. If you choose to forgive, there are many ways you can forgive this person; or these people, without ever condoning their actions. I suggest you do this work in your Sacred Space, privately.

- You can write a letter to them, and you never even have to send it.

- Tell them in the letter, or say what you feel out loud in words. Imagine them sitting in a chair far enough away from you so that you feel safe, and tell them what you need to tell them. Get it all out.

- If they are deceased you can still tell them everything you need to say to them. Speak the words. Tell them what you felt then. Be sure to tell them what you feel now.

- Some of these people may be in prison. You can imagine them there and a good, safe distance away from you. Let them know how you felt as the innocent child you were back then. Tell them what you know now. You are an adult and you are much stronger and wiser. Now, you are free to live as you choose.

This can take as much time as you need until you feel like you have gotten it out. There is really no right or wrong way to say what you feel inside. Just getting it all out is what's important here. Tell them what you need to say. If you choose to write it out in a letter, you can safely write it down and then rip it up, you can throw it all away or you can, in a very safe manner, burn it up. Let all that past fall away in the ashes. You can bury the ashes, or release them to the wind. Doing so would be an excellent way to symbolically put your past behind you. It is over and done with. It's dead, and it has no power over you any longer. To let it go means it has no power over you. If it still triggers you, you simply have not done the work and the trauma needs to be dealt with. Your past has no control over you unless you live there.

- Whatever you do, be sure to do so in a safe place and in a safe way. Never go looking for someone who is a threat to you still.

- Please allow the Police, and other authorities to handle that. Do not call them on the phone or use social media as a way to communicate with them. Be Smart and Be Safe!

- What you are doing here is also for you. You do not need to personally or virtually speak to them.

- You may have a personal relationship with them still, or you may not, because I do not know you or them personally and it is not in your best interests, or my own, to ever tell you what you should do, I say this: You can create the act of forgiveness simply by saying what you feel now, what you felt then, and how it all affected you. This decision is yours.

- Then, you can let your words go. You can end the attachment you have with them. This is what sets you free to create more happiness for yourself, for those you love, and for those people who truly love you and appreciate you.

The person or people who hurt you did so because of their dis-ease. They had to have been harmed somewhere in their lifetime in order to continue the cycle of abuse. This is NOT me condoning their horrific behavior. I will never do that. These people never received help, never received proper care and therapy for their pain and the abuses perpetrated against them, so the viscious cycles continued. I'm not making excuses for their terrible behavior. I'm simply understanding it. When you understand the why's, you can release the attachment your past has on you.

This is not an excuse for what they did to you. As adults we can utilize reason, logic and common sense to understand why. The inner child within us still does not understand. She/He still asks why? Why did this person hurt me and use me and leave me to pick up the pieces of my broken life and cause me to try, against all odds, to live as if I'm normal again?

The answers you seek are all right there inside of you. Allow your inner child to speak of her pain and any confusion she may have. Allow yourself to go deep and let her find her way back to the Adult you are now. Together you can walk this journey of Taking Back Your Power! It is our Egoic Mind that gets us into trouble. We Humans get really messed up when we allow the Ego to rule our thinking, doing and Be-ing. This is part of your Journey.

I have asked for and I have received Grace in my life. I have done the work, and I continue to do the work on myself. I listen to and ask for guidance from my Higher Self. The facts are that I have survived many abuses in my lifetime, as a little child, as a teen, and later as a woman expecting her first child. As a grown woman, living in another country I was nearly killed more than once, by a 6′ 4″ alcoholic, rugby playing, porn-addicted, Englshman. I use the term *man* loosely, he was not a man, chronologically he may have been. He behaved like a typical, and extremely drunk, teenage boy. I questioned his drinking and his treatment of me, and he did not like that. Since I have already wasted far too much of my precious Life Force Energy on him already, that's all I have to say. Please, do not waste your time here on this Earth with people who are not good for you, who mistreat you and who do not appreciate you for who you are. You Be Good Enough For Yourself.

These are my personal Spiritual beliefs about who and what we truly are. My beliefs are that we are not human beings having spiritual glimpses, or spiritual experiences every so often. We are Spiritual beings, a part of a Whole Divine Intelligence, and we are learning, growing and experiencing ourselves as Human Beings. There's a huge difference between the two. As Souls we are Perfect.

Your Soul Self is perfect. It is Absolutely Perfect and nothing can harm it. Nothing can kill it, and nothing can stop it from Be-ing. My Soul Self is perfect. It is absolutely Perfect, Whole and Complete in and of Itself. All of us, no matter where we live on this beautiful planet we call Earth, are Spiritual Beings.

The Human Self, not so much. The body dies. The human body can get sick and become dis-eased and it ages. The human mind can become ill. It can become stuck in the Egoic state. When we react to anything from our Ego, this is where we, as human beings, get into trouble. If we can silence the mental chatter in our minds, we can start to feel, and know a higher part of our Being. Our True Self.

The people who hurt you were doing so from that Egoic state. The True Self is pure Love. Pure Awareness of the

Whole. There is no hate, anger, perversion in that part of us. The All That Is, is that; ALL, and there is no ego in the ALL. Not one scintilla of a tiny fraction of an inch. Absolutely no ego. Everything that is judged, condemned, criticized, accosted, plagerised, stolen, raped and abused is done from a place, a mindset, of EGO. Again, this is not an excuse for what they did to you. We do much better when we put some perspective on the issues that so many of us face.

Somebody got to my father, just as somebody got to whoever it is that hurt you. Then my father took out his pain and confusion on my family and me. Your abuser took their pain and confusion, their hate and their frustrations out on you. As I asked for answers in understanding my Why's, I received my own personal answers. Just as you can too. When you ask for guidance, guidance shows up. Be still and your answers can come to you. We need to create the space for our answers to show up.

Meditation is an excellent way to do this. You don't have to sit in a Lotus position for this. You don't even have to burn incense if you don't want to or you are not comfortable with that. Personally, I love Incense, and I love burning sage. They purify the air and work to cleanse the energy in your Sacred Space and in your home. All you *really* have to do is to be quiet, for even just 5 minutes a day. Maybe you can stretch out that 5 minutes to 15 minutes a day. If you do this, you will start to find another side of you that you did not know even existed. This is the Real You. This is when you start to let go of that terrible past and you move forward, starting in your present moment on your Journey of Healing and this is how you start to Take Your Own Power Back. No matter what happened to you in your past, It is NOT Who You Are. Be Open minded about what I'm telling you here. Allow your own True Self to guide you.

Many of you complain about how unfair it was. Life is

not about fairness. Life does not give us experiences based on fairness. I remember feeling angry for years. I was so incredibly angry because I believed it wasn't fair. Fairness has nothing to do with any of it. Is it fair that someone boards a plane and goes happily and very excited to arrive on some exotic island for their hard-earned vacation, but the plane crashes and they are killed? Is it fair that some people are born blind? Is it fair that Earthquakes happen all over the world killing massive amounts of people and animals? Is it fair that Tsunamis often follow those devastating earthquakes, wiping out even more people and more animals, while destroying homes, buildings, and precious lives in the process? What happens when those disasters strike down the parents and care-takers of Innocent children? It is possible that many of them are taken to Orphanages, and some of those Orphanages are, allegedly, fronts for Human Trafficking. We can do better than this. We have to do better than this.

This is Life, and Life happens to all of us. Some people lose their mothers when they are just young children. Some people lose their beloved spouses, or partners. Some people lose their children. Some people are diagnosed with a serious disease just when they are ready to retire, and the list of Life's Challenges goes on and on. None of this is fair. Or, all of it is fair. Life, simply, just is.

The events of my life went full circle. Maybe this is the first time, in at least one of my lifetimes, where I actually got it right. Who knows, maybe I won't have to come back to this Earth School and suffer the slings and arrows, the push and the pulls and the immense joys followed by the deepest sorrows anymore. I don't know…I guess I'll just have to wait and see.

I came into this life and learned how to love, or at least what I thought was love. That love was usually always conditional. I'm still a work in progress. You are still a work in progress, I think we all are. Living as a human being is not easy. But then, that's what we are here for. We learn about ourselves, and in the process, maybe we discover our True Selves.

The person or people who hurt you did so because of their dis-ease. They had to have been harmed somewhere in their lifetime in order to continue the cycle of abuse. This is NOT me condoning their horrific behavior. I will never do that. However, my spiritual beliefs are such that I do believe the Man known as Jesus Christ lived and walked this Earth, and he spoke these words:

> *"Forgive Them Father, For They*
> *Know Not What They Do."*
>
> ~Jesus Christ

These people never received help. They never received care and therapy for their own pain and abuse. Perhaps they received very little in terms of after care and therapy. This is how the viscious cycles continue. The people who are Resilient, know there is something better and kinder. They are aware that a higher-level Love lives within them, and they choose to live their lives expressing the Light of God within. They seek to make the world a much better place for all and they start that journey by working on themselves first. Your ultimate goal here is to improve yourself. Not wasting your precious energy trying to change others.

I'm not making excuses for their terrible behavior. I'm simply understanding it. When you understand the why's, you can release the hold that your past has gripped upon you. Many of you constantly ask this question. Why? I asked myself that question for decades while I struggled to stay alive, and I have talked about this earlier in this book, but it bears repeating. The people who harmed you did not have control of their minds. They subconsciously became overwhelmed by the pain that they received, most likely as young children.

Our work is not finished just because you have read this book. Not unless you want it to be. I'm here and able to work with you as you continue on your own path of Self Dis-covery. I AM a Robbins-Madanes Trained Life Coach. I specialize in guiding my clients to Empower themselves after suffering childhood and/or domestic abuse. There is life after trauma, you just got lost in the pain of it all. It's okay, you are on your way back now.

Forgiveness is a lesson I learned the hard way, but I can honestly say to you all, that I did learn it. I came into this world loving my father, and I said goodbye to him as he left this world, after all those years of struggling in pain and with anger. After years upon years of suffering, I was able to let him go with all the love I could possibly have in my heart. My heart was filled with love. I knew full well what had happened in that room, yet none of it mattered in those three days, in those moments, as he was dying. All I could feel was forgiveness and love, and it was truly beautiful. I had that opportunity and thank God my sister had the sense to ask me to give him the morphine he needed. I wasn't sure if that was the proper thing for me to do, and yet, I certainly did do it for him, for my mother, my family and for Love. I did it for his Soul. I always believed that I must practice what Jesus Christ taught.

Chapter 19
FORGIVING HENRY

I MENTIONED TO YOU AT THE beginning of this book that I was raised as a Catholic. My father did not attend church services, and it is obvious to me now why he did not. My mother always attended church. I spent many Sundays attending Catholic church services. I enjoyed attending church very much. I also attended Catechism classes so I could receive my First Holy Communion. Then some years later; when I was older, I received my Holy Confirmation. All of these experiences and growth instilled one thing in particular within me, and that was the fact that Jesus Christ lived. Jesus was a Human Being who lived with Deep Awareness. I'm no religious scholar. I'm certainly no expert on the Bible. However, I do know this Truth. Jesus, a most beautiful, compassionate man, was completely Awake and He lived in Alignment of His True and Authentic Self. He lived this way even as a young child. He taught Forgiveness. If I learned anything from Jesus, it is that He taught us all through His very Life, Death and Life Again, that it is through the act of Forgiveness that we Connect with our True Divinity.

Please be careful to not confuse forgiveness with the act of condoning the harm that was done. Each one of us is a Divine Spiritual Being, we simply have forgotten who we are and we have disconnected, in a subconscious way, from our Divinity.

> "All people commit sins and make mistakes. God forgives them, and as people we are acting in a godlike (Divine) way when we forgive."

> ~An Essay on Criticism
> by Alexander Pope.

For most of my life, I have tried to live my life following the teachings of Jesus Christ.

It is not that I always considered myself a good, practicing Catholic, not by any means. As I became older, I pulled away from the Church, but I still held on to the teachings of Christ. Jesus Christ was one of the Greatest Teachers who ever walked this Earth. And while I still have much to learn from his teachings, I strive, every single day, to live my life as He taught. If I ever succeeded in getting one thing remotely right, it was committing an Act of Forgiveness for my Father and also for my Mother.

I remember having a conversation with my father after my second son was about 8-years old. My father and I were out for a drive in my car. Then we stopped somewhere, I don't remember exactly where, but in a parking lot, someplace where I could have the privacy to tell him what I wanted to say to him, without interruption.

I was telling him about how all the terrible things he did to me nearly killed me. He looked sort of surprised. He could not comprehend how any of what he did was harmful to me. In his mental illness, this ailment of his mind had convinced him that he was only loving me. He had hurt me so much over the years, that I had contemplated suicide many times, just to stop the pain.

People make the heartbreaking decision to commit suicide when they see no other way to escape their pain and put an end to their suffering. There is always another way to stop suffering! I do not believe suicide is the answer to any of our problems. I believe it will only cause us more pain in our next life. It will definitely cause the people whom we love and who love us, excruciating pain. I never wanted to die, I simply wanted a way for the constant feeling of not being good enough to go away. I wanted the belief that I was only *damaged goods* to forever leave my body-mind. I sought ways to Heal myself, and I wanted him to take some responsibility for what he had caused.

I remember feeling somewhat sorry for him, because he did not fully grasp what he had done. He said he was sorry. He did not mean to hurt me. He talked in that wimpy, weird voice he always had when he abused me for all those years. I had to end the conversation and go home. I could not take anymore of that voice. I hated that voice. I despised that creepy smirk he always had on his face. This gave me a stark warning that the Pedophille living in his Egoic Mind was still in control.

When he was dying, many years later, I felt empathy for him, and compassion. I wondered what must have happened to the Innocent, little boy, the impoverished boy, who struggled to save his widowed mother and his three younger brothers from starving to death. Sometimes, he and his brothers had to eat moldy tortillas, and at age 6, he sold newspapers on street corners to help his mother put food on the table and pay the bills. I don't know what happened to him, was he sexually abused? What caused him to find pleasure in sexually molesting his own daughter?

He never did tell me. I do know that the cycle of abuse stopped with me. He had no more daughters to hurt any longer. As I grew older and I grew stronger, it seemed that he grew younger and weaker. Funny how roles reverse over time. The servant becomes the master, so to speak.

I gave him his morphine suppositories, very carefully. I did not want to look at him, you know, down there. Not because I couldn't, but because I was very respectful of his right to die with dignity. He was, after all, a Soul too, living as a human being. He was a little boy who suffered things that probably made my suffering look like a walk in the park. I had only compassion and empathy and a deep desire to take away his pain – to serve him. I had nothing but forgiveness in my heart. I prayed over him. I sang to him. I brushed his hair, and I swabbed his dry mouth. I talked to him and told him it was ok, and I cried. I forgave him. It was important to me that he heard my words. This was not the only time I had told him that I had forgiven him. I had not one, single speck, not one scintilla, of anger or hatred for him.

I looked around the room where it all began. I remembered how I had rolled my eyes back and put my focus toward the window behind me and asked God to help me. I remembered how I begged God and Mother Mary, the Guardian Angels, the Saints and how I believed that no God intervened. No Virgin Mary saved me, no Saints or Apostles, no Creed was spoken, no Angels in white magically appeared to save this Innocent, frightened little girl, as she was forced to remain there on her parent's bed, helpless and all alone. No one heard at all, not even the chair.

I had it all wrong. It was in not intervening back then, that God was helping me. It was in not saving me that Mother Mary Blessed My Spiritual Growth. It was in holding silent and still Spiritual Witness, that the Saints allowed this child to be Authentic. It was in not appearing, that the Angels did appear. They were there, in that room, on the day I said my goodbyes, and I forgave him. All were there in the room as he died. All were there as the Innocent Child said goodbye to the Innocent Boy who was Henry.

I was in the moment. I was watching my father die. I was one of four people in that room. The room where I was sexually and psychologically abused by him. One of those people was dying. Again, the tears were streaming down my face, only this time it was for him, and not because of my pain. I prayed and I talked to him, I sang to him. I never left his bedside, until my brother insisted I go lay down in the other room for just a while.

I don't think it was much longer, before my brother came to wake me, and said it was happening. It was time. Our father, that man who seemed so big and strong to me as a young girl, was now so fragile, weak and quiet. It was all going to be over. That story of pain and heartache was nearing its end.

Then, as I spoke to him softly, and whispered in his ear, I forgive you, Dad. I love you, Dad. It's ok. It's all ok. Go to the Light. I'm OK now. You are free. The room was completely quiet. My brother stood next to me, our mother was near my Dad's side, but further back near his right knee. I was standing next to his face, and the room was all aglow. It was almost as if a fire was burning in a fireplace, but there was no fire, or as if there were candles lit, but there were no candles.

As I wept and offered prayers for the release of his Soul, I experienced an inexplicable phenomenon that felt like a Divine Blessing. It could be that my journey with him had gone full circle, or maybe it was because I had gained a deeper understanding of compassion, empathy, and unconditional love. Whatever the reason, what I saw was no illusion - IT was real.

I was not watching the clock. I was not timing what I witnessed. I can only guess at how long this went on for. It really doesn't matter to me anyhow. I know what I saw. I now *know* we are all more than just our physical bodies. I have known that for almost my entire life.

I will always believe what I believe this to be. People can try to make me wrong, or call me crazy, or whatever they choose. I was in that room, the room where I was so horribly treated by my own father. There was Grace in the room that day. The day my father, my abuser, died. My father became the source of my deepest pains and also the source of my greatest Joy! God IS Alive and Well. I have seen The Light of God with my own two eyes. Grace had entered the room. I saw It. I felt It. I experienced It. I Now Know IT.

As my Father passed on to his next Journey, I picked up our family Bible. I immediately read the 23rd Psalm. The 23rd Psalm is my very favorite of all the stories in the book of Psalms. I read it for him. I prayed for him to have peace. Many of us have experienced hurt and pain caused by others in our lives. It is often difficult to understand why someone would intentionally inflict harm on another person. I'm not suggesting that you must forgive. I'm simply telling you what happened for me.

I spoke at my father's funeral. His body lay in the casket, and it was draped with our U.S. flag. I stood up in a room packed full with hundreds of people who loved him. People whose lives he had helped to improve. People he helped in one way or another. He was always helping people. He was highly respected in the community. It was standing room only.

None of them knew the truth. Only a handful of people knew what had happened. Those people watched me as I spoke about him with such respect, compassion and pain over losing him. I did not want him to die, though I knew he would. He died almost 11 months to the day after my eldest sister died of breast cancer. I have always believed that if she would have gotten much better therapy, if someone could have helped her better with her pain, maybe we would not have lost her. When we lost her, I always knew he would follow shortly after her; his Soul would follow hers. They would be together again, and there truly are no tears in Heaven.

With the Grace of God... I let Henry go. No more shall he suffer. No more shall he cry out in hunger and fear, a poor boy, living without his father. Henry is loved now and forever more. As I write this very page of my story, it just so happens that today is my Father's birthday.

Happy Heavenly Birthday, Dad. I Love You, Always, XOXOXO

Research has shown that individuals who hurt others may have been victims of trauma or abuse themselves. This pain and suffering can create a cycle of abuse, as those who have been hurt continue to perpetuate that behavior onto others. Despite the daunting nature of this reality, there is always a Choice. You always have the Power to choose to continue the cycle of abuse or you can choose to stop it.

By acknowledging and understanding the root causes of hurtful behavior, we can begin to break the cycle of pain. Through acts of light and love, we have the power to transform darkness into healing, and with our healing, we live our Essence, our Light.

This requires effort and self-reflection, but it is possible to put an end to the destructive patterns that have plagued our lives and the lives of those around us. It is essential to recognize that this process is not easy and may require seeking help from others, such as a therapist, or a qualified Life Coach. With dedication and perseverance, we can heal ourselves and become agents of positive change in our communities. By doing the work to confront our own pain and the pain of those around us, we can create a brighter future for ourselves and future generations.

I think that maybe, just maybe, when we are completely pure of heart, when our compassion for another goes far beyond the call of duty. When we are completely at one with our Creator, God, The Universe, All That Is, Divine Intelligence, this is when miracles happen. This is when we are able to see through the eyes of Grace.

Grace appeared that day, because I was able to forgive the man who had wronged me. I'm not saying everyone can and should do that for their abusers. I was lucky. I was tested, my resolve was tested. I believe that I made the right decision for both myself and my father and we were both Blessed in the days and moments of his passing.

While my father had emotionally, physically and sexually abused me, he had loved me in the only way he knew how, and he did love me. He did not love himself. Many children aren't so lucky. My father did not break my bones, or throw me up against a wall and bash my head in. He never did the horrific things that some children are subjected to. I was physically hurt, yes, but not violently beaten, locked up, chained to a bed and nearly starved to death as some children are.

Grace is always with us. We just have to look. We just have to be fully in the present moment. That is something very few human beings are able to do. We are conditioned to allow our Egoic mind to control everything we think, say and do. We lose ourselves in the acts of being human. We become attached, and rightfully so, to our families, our careers, our homes, our belongings, and yet, we really don't own any of these people and things. One thing is for certain in life, and that is death. If you are alive right now, and how could you be reading this book if you weren't alive, one thing is for sure, you will die at some point. Every single one of us have that in common with each other. We all have our births and we will all have our deaths. It is what we do between those two events that really matter.

I do not believe in mistakes. I believe in learning experiences. A person can be highly educated, and yet still behave like a complete fool. A person can have little in the way of education, and yet posess incredible intelligence, especially when it comes to common sense. How many Master degrees a person holds does not in any way prove their intelligence. How they treat others, definitely does. Our intelligence would be better measured in terms of how well we love. How do we treat our fellow human beings and the animals sharing this beautiful planet with us?

How well do we treat our loved ones? Why are we so

critical of each other? Why do we seem to lack patience and empathy? I believe it is because we are either living in our past, stuck in our past experiences and being trapped by our memories, or we are too worried about the future and what it holds in store for us. I believe that there was no other place for me to go on the day of my father's death. I was done with the past. I was not going to have him in my future, because he was at that very moment leaving the Earth. The only moment I had was there as His Soul left his body and he detached from his Egoic Mind. All that was left was Pure Soul. His Soul chose to be my father, and my Soul chose to be his daughter. That's going to be a very tough pill to swallow, for some of you who are so used to choosing to hang on to your Victim Mentality. That's ok. It won't stop me from speaking and writing about what I know to be True.

When, and if, in this lifetime, you come to the realization that you are so much more than the story you tell yourself. If you realize that you're actually a Soul having a Human Experience, and it's not the other way around, then you can understand my words.

To be Self-Actualized is the greatest knowledge of all. There is no other intelligence, no degrees, no book smarts, no Ivy League School that can teach you the Truth of Who and What You Truly Are. There is no priest, no clergy person, no scientist, no human being living on this planet who can hand your True Self over to you. I cannot give IT to you. I can only guide you to the steps you must take to find Yourself. Because Your True Self doesn't come from outside of you. It is already Within You. You, and you alone, must do the work. You, and you alone, must find Yourself. When you find IT, you will know... and always remember:

- **It was never true what they said to you.**

- **You are not the sum of all the terrible things that happened to you.**

- **It was never true. None of it Is Your Authentic Truth.**

Some of you may be wondering, well what is my Authentic Truth, Marie? What I can say, in total and complete confidence to you, is this: When you continue asking, you shall receive. When you keep living in the present moment and stop focusing on your past, your Authentic Truth happens – It unfolds and manifests in ways that will change your life forever. Do imagine your compelling future, just don't stress over what has not shown up as your present moment. Always be Humble, Kind and Grateful. The Reality is, your Higher Self was never actually lost in the first place. You simply have not been paying attention to It. Your Egoic Mind is where you placed your attention, as a result of the trauma you experienced. Then you stayed stuck in that state. Your Higher Self has and always IS Your Authentic Truth.

You were lied to and then you believed those lies. Those lies eventually became your Identity. But, here's the thing, all lies eventually crumble and fall apart. All lies are built on unstable ground. They only stick around because you have held on to them. They are not your Truth. They are not you. They are all based on the lies that others fed you, because those people believed the lies someone else had said to them. You have become a part of the pattern. If there is one thing I know about patterns it's that all patterns can be changed. As you look at your patterns, you can decide for yourself whether or not those patterns are positive or negative.

Ask yourself, are my patterns helping me, and are they helping the people I love? Is the world as a whole a much better place to live in, because I AM Authentic? Ask yourself, Am I still holding on to negative patterns that are disturbing my peace of mind, my health, my finances and that are creating my unhappiness, as well as the unhappiness of others?

These people who hurt you did so from their own suffering. They could only give you what had been done to them, on one level or another. They did not learn Love. They learned how to Take. You ask, What is "take," Marie? They learned how to *take* because others had taken from them. They kept the cycle of abuse going in their family. Some of it went on for generations.

The patterns you have been living are, most likely, not even your own. They were taught to you. You buried them deep within your own psyche. The body and mind are not separate. What has been accepted as Truth in your mind becomes ingrained into your body. Your health and your subsequent happiness suffer for it. You don't even realize that you are running on automatic pilot. This continuous looping of false beliefs about yourself keeps going around and around your thinking process, ultimately causing you to not see the forest for the trees. You do not see the happiness and joy you can truly experience for the pain and anger you hold onto.

I could go on and on about what child abuse and domestic abuse does to your health. My guess is that you probably have some experience with that. I'm sure you have suffered headaches, migraines, anxiety, depression, frequent colds, maybe asthma and pneumonia, possibly even cancer; and you know deep within you where it all started from. Not that those ailments and very serious diseases are not real. Oh, they are definitely real, and they can and do kill. I believe we open ourselves up to illness and disease when our thoughts repeatedly remain negative. Especially when we stuff all that negativity down deep within ourselves. Thoughts truly are things and what we believe about ourselves becomes materialized in one form or another as our reality.

YOU MUST STAND GUARD AT THE DOORWAY TO YOUR MIND!

The hurtful things they said and did to you were never yours to begin with. You just happened to be in the exact right place at the exact right time. If it wasn't you, it would have been someone else. It was you though, and it doesn't matter the amount of time that has passed since the traumatic events happened. Taking your Authentic Power back can happen for you at any time. IT IS NEVER TOO LATE. You have forgotten who you are, and once you make the clear decision to break those patterns, to look at and feel what you have been repeating and holding onto because someone else took advantage of you, you have started the process of re-connection and awakening.

Your Higher Self has never left you. It is impossible for that to happen, unless you are no longer alive. That could not happen unless you were dead. So, to be Truly Alive, to be Truly Aware, means you can and must reconnect to who you Truly Are. This is something only you can do for yourself. I cannot do it for you, because I'm not living your life. I have my own life to live and you have yours. I have my own Soul, my own Authentic, Higher Self and you have yours.

Are you thinking, but Marie, how do I do this? Do I pray? Do I go to Church? Do I have to be Religious? Do I have to meditate on top of a mountain somewhere in Nepal, and stop eating meat? The answer to all of those questions is a resounding No. You only have to ask. Ask. Just simply ask your Authentic Self to guide you in letting go of all that crap that happened back then, and to give you the strength and the courage to put one foot in front of the other and Be Whole again. You see, everything you need is already within you. All you need to do is to Ask.

While you do not have to attend church services to know your True Self, I find attending services, mediations, singing praise to our creator to be very inspiring. Being with other like-minded people is always good for the Soul.

When you ask to be shown what is Divine within you, and it is Divine, The Divine answers your call. IT doesn't say, *well I would like to show you who you truly are, but you know, you aren't really worthy of that yet. You really did some bad stuff back then, and I saw you flip that person off the other day because they cut you off in traffic.* That's never gonna happen. God, the Universe, All That IS, has no choice in the matter. ITs job is in Waking You Up! IT's in making you Awake and Aware of who you truly are.

Everything that went on back then, is really of no consequence, not when it comes to being your Authentic Self. Choosing to stay stuck in your pain, in your heartaches, in your triggers, in your nightmares... angry and complaining about how you were wronged and defending your right to hold onto all your anger and rage; that loneliness and sadness and ultimately the anxiety and depression that follows, it all keeps you living like a hostage in your own mind and it continues, for as long as you continue to hold onto it. All of it keeps you disconnected from your Truth.

"You do not attract what you want. You attract who you are."

~ Dr. Wayne W. Dyer

Have you noticed the patterns I have created for you as you read this book? If I have repeated some key points within these pages, it is on Purpose. Your mind/body is like a computer. What goes in must come out. If you continue to keep feeding your mind false beliefs about who you are and why you are here, you will live that, and you will continue to attract that.

The goal for us all is to create significant change for ourselves, and ultimately, for those we love, who wish they could help us, but they simply do not know how. We human beings can create significant, life-affirming, positive change for ourselves and others, if we simply make the decision to do so. Once you make up your mind to Take Your Own Unique Power Back, God, Infinite Intelligence will do the rest.

You only have to make the space. It is a Sacred Space you are creating. When you acknowledge that there is more to who you are, regardless of your past, you surrender all your pain and all your hatred, no matter how justified you may feel in it. You change your vibration. You open up your mind/body to the Divinity Within. It isn't something you are trying to force within you. You are not taking something that exists outside of yourself. It is already a part of you. This is exactly what Jesus Christ taught. He taught us that The Kingdom of Heaven IS Within You.

"You Do Not Need A Near Death
Experience To Know The Grace of
God. All You Have To Do Is Pay
Attention. The Signs Are Everywhere."

~ Marie Castellano

Chapter 20

I SAW THE LIGHT AND THE LIGHT IS GOOD

I HAVE TAKEN YOU ON A journey, you have seen into my past, you have been with me in my now, and you have, metaphorically, walked in my shoes, albeit for a short while. There are three very important messages I AM giving you in this book and if you have any takeaways, I pray that they are these:

1. **You Are NOT Alone.** You Will Never Be Alone, because you are created by the Light. When it is time, your body will cease living, but YOU will return to the whole of the Light. Whether you believe in God, Jesus, Krishna, Buddha, or The Spirit In The Sky, You and I are parts of the Whole that IS Light. That Light has Intelligence, within. IT IS Intelligence. IT IS KNOWING. I call IT, Divine Intelligence. You may also hear people refer to IT as the Collective.

2. **Divine Intelligence Is Within You.** I'm not talking about your IQ numbers here. It does not matter how many initials you have after your name. How much money you have, or how little you have. Every single sentient being living on this Earth has been created and lives with the Intelligence of the Light within them. The Light is who you truly are. You are a Soul having a Human experience. At some point your body will cease to live. Your Soul, however, is infinite. IT goes on and on and on and on. Divine Intelligence Is You.

3. **There Are No Accidents.** Even accidents are not accidents. There is a message, a learning, a growth and a Purpose that your Light, your Inner Intelligence, your Higher Self, Your Authentic Self is guiding you to experience and know. When you ask for answers as to why these supposed accidents and horrific things happened to you, in your asking, you shall receive answers. *Ask and Ye Shall Receive*[11]. I don't know what your receiving will look like, because that is your own unique journey. I do know that if you Ask with humbleness, with sincerity and an open heart, you are heard and you shall receive your knowledge. This is your gift, and it belongs to nobody but you. The question is will you ask?

So many people think they have Life all figured out. They possess money and own beautiful, comfortable homes and they value their self-worth based on how much money they have. They, for all sense and purposes, according to the Happiness Gurus, have everything a person could ever want

[11] "Matthew 7:7–8 - Wikipedia." https://en.wikipedia.org/wiki/ Matthew_7:7%E2%80%938. Accessed 22 Jul. 2023.

and need. And yet, some of the wealthiest people on the planet are miserably unhappy, many even suicidal. Why is that?

Most people believe their worth to be the dollar amount in their checking and savings accounts and in their 401(k). Most of us value our worth, our sense of worthiness, and thus our happiness, based on how much money we have that allows us to live our lives in the way of our choosing. Yes, having enough money to put a roof over your head and food on the table, to be able to buy clothes, go on exciting and relaxing vacations, and to travel the world are all wonderful, amazing experiences. To not work at a J-O-B you loathe, is definitely financial freedom and it gives you freedom to choose how you will live your life, and how you choose to spend your very precious time, which is your most precious commodity, after excellent health. You can't have time if you do not have your health.

Ultimately, everything that money can buy or not buy, is teaching you lessons. To learn the lessons on this Earth that your Soul chose are, and will always be, your true purpose in this one particular life of yours. I believe that after this one, another, and maybe another. You will probably have relationships with other people who are closest to you now. You may be in different roles, but the Souls are the same. More lessons to learn, and the lessons you learned in your other lives, you will not have to learn again. You have graduated from those Life Classes, and so you move on up until you no longer need to reincarnate again. Welcome to Earth School, May You Learn Your Lessons Well, and Remember, Life Is But A Dream!

What I Believe NOW:

I believe that as babies we are pure Innocence – that is we have a spotless slate – we are in essence, pure. We have not developed our sense of human-self yet, we are devoid of Egoic Mind. We have not yet said anything hurtful to anyone to feel guilty about. We have not climbed up to the cookie jar and stolen cookies and then tried to lie about our actions when we were found out. We are entirely guilt free. We are Pure Innocence and Pure Love. I firmly believe that if babies had the ability to speak they would be able to communicate who they were in their past life, and even why they are here now.

Then at some point in your life – everything changed – you experienced pain, and your experience with human contact was not one of love and tender, gentle care. As a baby, or very young child, your beautiful, pure, clean slate had been tarnished. Maybe you received love and tender care from one person and yet another may have been the sick individual who did you harm. You were powerless to stop the abuse. You were so tiny, helpless, and perhaps you were not even talking yet. Some of you were so young that you were not able to walk. Running away was not an option for you. Screaming about what was happening, and by whom, was not an option. All you could do was cry. Your defense mechanisms kicked in, your subconscious mind did its job and your Ego-self was created, that's not a bad thing. You were protected by your mind's ability to compartmentalize your memories, even when you were that young, and especially when you were so young, because it was your only defense.

Your Subconscious mind does its work and it blocks out your painful experiences, your painful memories. You survived, because you forgot what was far too overwhelming for your young, Innocent self to remember. Defense mechanisms of the mind have their purpose. This is true, however, you don't want to stay stuck in them. Let them serve their initial purpose and then move on. Otherwise, you will remain lost in the trauma of your past.

"CHANGE HAPPENS WHEN YOU REALIZE YOU HAVE THE CAPACITY TO CHOOSE"

~ Tony Robbins

Consider your past experiences, your current circumstances, and your hopes for the future. Ask yourself what you want to achieve, what kind of person you want to be, and what legacy you want to leave behind. By answering these questions honestly and thoughtfully, you can gain a better understanding of what drives you and what you need to do to achieve your goals. Knowing your why is a powerful tool that can help you overcome obstacles, stay committed to your goals, and live a more fulfilling life. So take the time to explore your motivations and values, and discover the path that will lead you towards the life you truly desire.

Personal growth and fulfillment are undoubtedly among the most critical pursuits in life. However, achieving these goals can prove challenging, especially without a clear sense of purpose guiding our efforts. This is where the idea of identifying your "why" comes into play. The concept of "why" refers to the underlying reason behind everything we do. It's the driving force that motivates us, gives us direction, and helps us navigate life's twists and turns.

For some people, their "why" might be to overcome emotional pain, while for others, it might be to attain genuine happiness or gain a deeper understanding of themselves, thus allowing them Peace. No matter what your "why" might be, the key is to always keep it at the forefront of your mind. This means taking the time to reflect on your motivations regularly, and making sure that your actions align with your overarching goals. By doing so, you can ensure that you're staying true to yourself and moving towards the life you truly want to lead.

Of course, identifying your "why" isn't always easy. It requires a deep level of introspection and self-awareness, which can be challenging to cultivate. However, the rewards of doing so are immeasurable. By identifying your "why," you can gain a sense of clarity and purpose that will help you make more meaningful decisions, overcome obstacles, and ultimately lead a more fulfilling life. Identifying your "why" is one of the most fundamental aspects of achieving personal growth and fulfillment. By taking the time to understand your motivations and keeping them front and center in your mind, you can gain a sense of direction and purpose that will help you navigate life's challenges with confidence and resolve.

There are far too many people to list here who have found themselves in despair at one point in their lives, yet they overcame Life's obstacles and created not only huge success for themselves, but went on to contribute the wealth of their knowledge in service to the world. If people such as Louise Hay, Dr. Wayne Dyer, Byron Katie, Oprah Winfrey, Tony and Sage Robbins, Martin Luther King, Jr., Eckhart Tolle, Gabor Mata, Dean Graziosi and Dr. Joe Dispenza (just to name a few) can do it, so can you. There is nothing stopping you, except the stories you tell yourself. Feed your Soul. Never feed your Egoic Mind.

Childhood abuse is a devastatingly common reality that affects millions[12] of people around the world. It is highly likely those numbers are over a billion.

For those who have endured such trauma, the idea

---

[12] "Violence against children - World Health Organization (WHO)." 29 Nov. 2022, https://www.who.int/news-room/fact-sheets/detail/violence-against-children. Accessed 5 Oct. 2023.

of breaking the cycle can often feel like a distant dream. However, despite the difficulties that lie ahead, it is imperative that we have open and honest conversations about this issue. By staying silent, you only perpetuate the harm that has already been inflicted upon you. It is important to understand that silence is not golden in cases of childhood abuse. When you keep your stories hidden and shielded from the Light, you allow your pain and suffering to fester and grow.

Doing this can make you vulnerable to remaining stuck in your emotions and your feelings. If you stay stuck long enough in your hatred, anger, frustration, shame, blame, pain, and your beliefs that you are Not Worthy of anything good in your Life, you are not standing guard at the doorway of your mind. This is how childhood abuse survivors turn their backs and their minds away from all that is Good. This is where Egoic Mind takes control manifesting all those painful emotions and beliefs out into the world and your pain-body[13] is created.

We need to acknowledge the truth of what happened to us so that we can begin to heal. Telling our stories can be difficult, but it is an essential part of the healing process[14]. Not only does it allow us to confront the pain and trauma we've experienced, but it also helps to raise awareness of the issue and creates a sense of solidarity among survivors. Sharing our experiences can help to break down the barriers of shame and isolation that so often accompanies childhood abuse. In short, breaking the cycle of childhood

---

[13] "How to Identify and Stop Your Pain-Body | A New Earth - YouTube." 27 Apr. 2014, https://www.youtube.com/watch?v=Fzj7R9IB48s. Accessed 5 Oct. 2023.

[14] "A New Earth: The Pain Body (Chapter 5) Oprah's Super Soul." https://podcasts.apple.com/us/podcast/a-new-earth-the-pain-body-chapter-5/id1264843400?i=1000429115655. Accessed 5 Oct. 2023.

abuse requires us to speak out and break the silence. It is only through the power of our collective voices that we can hope to create a brighter future for ourselves and for future generations.

FIND SOMETHING YOU CARE ABOUT
MORE THAN YOUR PAIN AND MAKE
THAT CAUSE YOUR PURPOSE!!

Clean up the oceans from plastic pollution, volunteer at your place of worship, help the elderly in your community. Do you love animals? Then volunteer at your local animal shelter. Donate clothes and supplies in your community for the homeless and those suffering from domestic and/or childhood abuse. Pray and meditate for yourself and those you love. Pray and meditate to end human suffering NOW.

TAKE YOUR PAIN And TURN IT INTO YOUR CAUSE!

Marie Castellano

The Truth Behind My Father

As a little girl, I idolized my father. My family and I had this standing joke, it wasn't really a joke, so much as we just sort of rolled our eyes in unison as we chuckled in like mind, because our father was repeating himself again. He liked to tell his WWII stories, and he would tell them to any ears that would listen. Most of the time, when I was very young, those ears would be mine.

I was a bit of a *TomBoy* growing up, and I was very tough. I ran track in school. I definitely had no interest in sewing, and I was not artistic at all. I could ride a horse, barrel race, and jump. I loved to ride and race horses with my friends. We would ride everywhere we could find the land to let the horses rip and run full speed as fast as their strong legs would carry them.

I also loved to listen to my Dad's war stories, at least I did when I was young, during my Elementary School years. He was always filming us kids, my Mom and other family members who would come to visit. He filmed us at Knotts Berry Farm, Disneyland, and while camping in Northern CA, under the giant Sequoias, we had some very good times back then.

He would eagerly display his collection of distinguished medals earned during his time serving in World War II. The proud glimmer in his eyes as he filmed me securely grasping his Purple Heart spoke volumes. My dad was a hero in my innocent eyes. The deep scar on his back was all the proof I needed. During the war, he had been hit by Bazooka shrapnel. Although I was only a young child, and I lacked a deeper understanding of the vast historical context, I absorbed the gravity of his message. Which were the atrocities committed by the notorious figure, Adolf Hitler, who indiscriminately took the lives of countless innocent men, women and children solely based on their religious beliefs and their racial backgrounds. This realization served as a poignant reminder of the senseless violence that plagued humanity during those dark times.

My Dad and I would sit next to each other on the carpet in our living room. My Mother sat in her rocking chair, and together we watched WWII movies. The Bridge On The River Kwai, Patton, The Dirty Dozen, The Great Escape, Stalag 17, From Here To Eternity, The Caine Mutiny, and the list goes on and on. I imagined my Father to be as heroic as the heroes in these films. I always felt safe and very protected when my 6′ 2″ Dad was near. If I was frightened by anyone or anything, he was the safe place I would run to.

That is what a Father should be. They should be our protectors, our leaders, our guides, and their principles and their values should be of good, strong, moral judgment. A father should be loving and kind, but also be willing to show his children he is capable of feeling other feelings such as sadness, even fear at times. A father shows his children that he is an equal to his wife, spouse, or partner, and that both of this child's parents (if living in a two parent home) are on an equal playing field.

If only we could break the cycle of childhood abuse. Maybe one day, my wish will come true. We must have this conversation. We have already been harmed. The only thing that can hurt us now is remaining silent. Silence is Not Golden. Not in this instance. We can tell our stories, if for no other reason, to keep the energy of the pain and the heartache from settling in our cell tissue, our bones, our hearts and minds. Then, we can set it all aside. It's over and done with and we do ourselves no good continuing the conversation. This is the reason I wrote this book.

I'm getting my story out and I AM Aware that by reading it, You, My Dear Reader, can gather enough courage and strength to tell yours. Never keep it all locked inside you. Never wait for those apologies you may never receive. Then, you too, can move forward, and set that part of your past aside. Let it remain in the past, where it belongs, as you live your present moment and create the life of your dreams.

Always remember: It is Not your past that you are stuck in. It is your THOUGHTS about your past that is traumatizing you. When you notice a thought about your past abuse starting to rear its ugly head, stop and take back your POWER! You control your Thoughts, it is not the other way around unless you choose to stay there!

Say to yourself these words: I NOW Live My Life In The Present Moment! I Choose What Thoughts I Keep and those thoughts that serve me no purpose, but to suffer. I CAN Choose to Suffer, or I CAN Choose to HEAL. I CHOOSE MY RIGHT TO HEAL. THE PAST IS OVER and DONE WITH. I CHOOSE TO LIVE NOW!!!

Your "trauma" is not reliving your past, that's impossible to do. Your "triggers" are the thoughts you hold onto. Your past is no longer happening. You are reliving your thoughts about your past. Thoughts can be changed. This does not mean the past you lived through did not happen, of course it did. What it does mean is that you are in control of your own healing. No one keeps you living in a mental prison with your past, but you. When you Realize this Truth, You begin to Take Your POWER BACK!!!

IN LOVING MEMORY OF LOUISE HAY

"Remember, you have been
criticizing yourself for years,
and it hasn't worked. Now
work on approving yourself
and see what happens."

~Louise L. Hay

I remember the first time I saw Louise Hay. I was attending my very first Whole Life Expo, in Los Angeles, CA where I'm from. I was born and raised in Southern California. This event was huge. I'm walking with my older brother and taking in all the sights and the delightful smells while watching so many interesting looking people. There was a lot of incense and sage burning, and blissful aromas from yummy body oils, and slowly burning candles that were everywhere. The place was filled with happy, smiling faces.

I believe this was one of, if not the, very first Whole Life Expo. We were walking on one of the main Los Angeles Convention Center's aisles. There was a group of people walking together heading in our direction. I looked over in their direction and I noticed a tall, slender woman who was surrounded on all sides by people. She had very blonde hair about shoulder length. I remember her looking across past the people on either side of her. She looked directly at me and she did not look away, she looked almost as if she knew me, at least, that's what it felt like to me. She smiled at me and it was a very knowing smile; a very confident smile. This was the very first time I saw Louise Hay. She was the Keynote Speaker. I hung on her every word. She had such a presence. Her voice was soft, and kind, yet her words were strong, confident, all knowing and very powerful.

Over the many decades that followed, I continued to study and learn everything I could from Louise Hay. I started reading her books, I listened to her tapes and cds. I would attend her workshops and seminars. Money was always one thing I struggled with having enough of and it was Louise Hay who taught me how to change my thoughts and beliefs about money and God. She taught me that I could, in fact, Heal myself from the pain of childhood sexual abuse.

She will always hold a very special place in my Heart and Soul. Thank You, Louise

XO

IN LOVING MEMORY OF DR. WAYNE DYER

*"If you don't make peace
with your past, it will keep
showing up in your present."*

~Dr. Wayne Dyer

I purchased my very first Dr. Wayne Dyer book when I was just 18 years old. I rented an apartment for myself and my baby boy, who was still quite young and was still sleeping in his crib. I could not afford a 2 bedroom apartment. My son's crib, his chest of drawers, and all his toys and clothes were set up in his bedroom. I slept on a pull-out couch in the living room. This was the best I could do with the little bit of money I earned.

I worked at a store, just next door, so I walked to work. There was a very nice, kind and caring family living in the apartment building next to mine and the mother babysat and took excellent care of my son while I was away at work. I worked as a cashier.

I have always loved books. I still have some of my

childhood books. I kept them in excellent condition, until my youngest son took a crayon to some of them one day, many years later. I never had any interest in romance novels, or smut stories as I liked to call them. My interests were always in reading Self-Help books. I was a voracious reader. If I wasn't away checking people in and out of my checkstand, or I wasn't cooking dinner and changing my son's diapers, giving him his bath and tucking him in his little crib at night, I was probably reading a book. I read everything I could get my hands on that would help me to help myself overcome the obstacles that living with my parents had given me.

One of those very first books was Your Erroneous Zones by Dr. Wayne W. Dyer.

I devoured Wayne's words as if they were food for my hungry Soul. And, they were! Wayne kept me alive, in a sense. Wayne gave me hope, when I thought I had none left. Wayne spoke to my very heart and soul. I remember taking that book with me everywhere I went. Being a Southern California Girl, and loving the beach as much as I do, I would take my son to the beach, usually Santa Monica, Malibu, Will Rogers, Venice or Zuma, so he could play in the sand, have fun learning how to ride the waves and enjoy the California sunshine. We would build sandcastles together, eat the sandwiches, fruits and snacks I packed, and he would play with his cars and trucks after lunchtime while I would read *Your Erroneous Zones*. People would see me reading, or carrying the book, and ask me about it, and with much passion I would tell them what it was about. Wayne's beautiful inspiring works helped them just as they did me. I continued reading, watching and learning all I could from the beautiful man he was.

Wayne, Thank you for inspiring me
to never give up and to
See the Light that Shines so Bright
in every person I meet.

XO

> "Forgiveness Is An Attribute
> of The Strong"
>
> ~Mahatma Gandhi

AN ACT OF FORGIVENESS

So many women ask me about forgiveness. The other "F" word as I like to call it. They find it extremely difficult to forgive those who have hurt them, and why wouldn't they? Forgiveness is something you grow into. You cannot just say the words, I forgive you, great that's done, without having forgiveness within yourself to truly mean those words. If you are trying to say what you think you are supposed to say, because doing that will only add to your belief that you are not being good enough. Your Heart and Soul know when you are faking it. Work on yourself first. Don't go trying to forgive others until you have learned how to forgive yourself first. This is important.

> You cannot give away something that
> you don't already own for yourself.
> It's impossible. Divine Intelligence
> Does Not Work That Way.

This also reminds me of why so many young girls, and not so young women (this is all true for boys and men too) will give themselves away in the hopes of being loved. I did this over and over again. I was a young woman who was trying to replace the love of her Father. I needed to feel loved again. I needed to feel safe again. It made me a young woman who wanted something to call her own. Something, or someone, that nobody could take from me, and so, I set out looking for that love in all the wrong places. What was the result of all my pain and suffering? It was eventually transformed into Compassion, Empathy and Resilience. Because I never gave up. I'd get knocked down and I always picked myself back up. I asked God to teach me what I most needed to learn. I repeatedly said these words: "Lord, make me an instrument of Your peace."[15]

I was in the moment. I was watching my father die. I was one of four people in that room, and one of those four people was dying. That room where I was sexually and psychologically abused by him for so many years. Yet again, the tears were streaming from my face, only this time they were tears of empathy and love for him and not about my pain. I prayed for him. I talked to him. I sang to him. I never left his bedside. I remained at his bedside enveloping him in Forgiveness for 3 days and 3 nights. Until my Brother insisted I go lie down on the bed, in another room for just a while.

I don't think it was much longer, before my brother came to wake me, and said it was happening. It was time. Our father, the man who seemed so big, powerful and strong to me as a young girl, was now so fragile, weak and quiet. He was dying. It was all going to be over. My story of pain and heartache was nearing its end.

Then as I spoke to him softly, and whispered in his ear, I forgive you Dad. I love you Dad. It's ok. It's all ok. Go to the

---

[15] "Most Powerful Prayer of Saint Francis of Assisi - Psalm 91." http://psalm91.com/make-me-an-instrument-a-prayer-of-saint-francis-of-assisi/. Accessed 5 Oct. 2023.

Light. I'm OK now. You are free. The room was completely quiet. My brother stood next to me, our mother was near my Dad's side, but further back near his right knee. She did not speak. I was standing next to his face, and the room was all aglow. It was almost as if a fire was burning in a fireplace, but there was no fire. Or, as if there were candles lit, but there were no candles.

As I cried softly, and prayed for his Soul to be freed at last, I witnessed something I can only say was a gift from God. Maybe it was because I had completed the full circle with him. Maybe it was because I had learned what it meant to be truly compassionate, to be empathetic, to Love, Absolutely Unconditionally. Maybe it was because I had always strived to live my life, as best as I could, keeping in mind the lessons Jesus The Christ taught. What I witnessed was no mirage. It was not something I made up. It was not something I was hoping for. It was not coming from my imagination. It was not coming from my stressful thoughts at the time. I was enveloped in Peace. I was in the Moment. Completely in this beautiful, perfect, Real and Present moment. As I stood there next to my Father, I saw this haze almost, a movement of what I can only believe was my father's Soul being released from the constraints of ITs human attachment to my father's body.

I know that's going to shock some of you, but it's exactly what happened. I watched and there was no sound coming from It. I saw this upward moving Light, almost like a glitter, but not sparkly like glitter. It's hard to describe, because I have never seen anything like this before or after that day. I have been at the bedside of other people whom I loved who were passing or had just passed away. I never witnessed anything like this before or after.

I looked up at the window blinds in the room to make sure what I was witnessing was not light streaming in from the light outside. I knew it wasn't, but I looked just the same. I saw the Light, and the Light Was Good. That was all I needed to know at the moment. If I attempt to put mere English words to IT to describe the color, size and texture, I would have to say IT was almost gold in color. There were far too many not quite circles above his face and chest to count, and IT appeared to hover over my father's heart and chest area, very slowly. IT moved upward, but not as you might think from watching movies or maybe reading about in books. IT did not move up toward the windows or the ceiling in that room. IT did have a very slight motion, and slowly moved, not all at once, gradually, moving bit by bit as I watched without moving a muscle, as it just vanished right in front of me, right in the space above him. They say every cloud has a silver lining… my lining was gold.

I was not watching a clock, and was not timing what I witnessed. I can only guess at how long this went on, minutes. It really doesn't matter to me anyhow. I know what I saw. I know we are all more than just our physical bodies. I have known that for my entire life. I will always believe what I Know this to be. People can try to make me wrong, or call me crazy, or whatever they choose. It doesn't matter to me the judgments of others. I know what I saw, and what I saw was GOOD and IT was LIGHT.

I was in that room, the room where I was so horribly treated by my own father, and there was Grace in the room those 3 Miraculous Days. The day my father, my hero and my captor; my abuser, died. My father became the source of my deepest pain and also my greatest Joy! God IS Alive and Well. I have seen the part of who we truly are as the Collective, the Light, with my own two eyes. Grace had entered the room. I saw It. I felt It, and I understood It.

As my Father passed on to his next Journey, I picked up our family Bible. I immediately read the 23rd Psalm. The

23rd Psalm is my very favorite of all the stories in the book of Psalms. I read it for him. I prayed for him to have peace.

The people who have hurt us in our lives did so because they have been hurt themselves. They have been hurt so badly that they continue to keep the cycle of pain and abuse going, as they inflict that pain on others. Our LIGHT and LOVE can put an end to that Darkness forever. We must do the work.

I think that maybe, just maybe, when we are completely pure of heart, when our compassion for another goes far beyond the call of duty. When we are completely at one with our creator, God, The Universe, All That Is, that is when miracles happen. Then we are able to see through the eyes of Grace. I know Grace came to me on that day, because I was able to forgive the man who had wronged me. I'm not saying everyone can and should do that for their abusers. I was lucky. While my father had emotionally, physically and sexually abused me for many years, he had loved me in the only way he knew how and he did love me.

Many children aren't so lucky. My father did not break my bones, or throw me up against a wall and bash my head in. He never did the horrific things that some children go through. I was physically hurt, yes, but not as horrifically as some children are. We must pay attention and educate ourselves to the Evil that is Human Trafficking and Organ Harvesting. It is up to us to stop it for once and for ALL.

Grace is always with us. We just have to look. We have to be fully in the present moment, living our Presence. This is something very few human beings are able to do, because most are living their lives on automatic pilot. We are so conditioned to allow our Egoic minds to control everything we think, say and do. We lose ourselves in the actions of being human. We become attached, and rightfully so, to our families, our careers, our homes, our belongings and yet, we really don't own any of these people and things. One thing is for certain in life, and that is death. If you are alive right now, and how could you be reading this book if you weren't alive? One thing is for sure, you will die at some point. Every single one of us have that in common with each other. We all have our births and we will all have our deaths. It's what we do between those two events that really matters.

I don't believe in mistakes. I believe in learning experiences. A person can be highly educated, and yet still behave like a complete fool. A person can have little in the way of education, and yet possess incredible intelligence, especially when it comes to common sense. How many degrees a person holds does not in any way prove their intelligence. How they treat others, definitely does. Our intelligence would be better measured in terms of how well we love and how well we appreciate life. What are you grateful for? How do you treat your fellow human beings who walk this planet with you? The animals, birds, insects, forests, oceans, rivers, lakes and streams sharing this beautiful planet with you, do you take them for granted? It's time to be honest with yourself. If you can't be honest with yourself, you cannot be honest with anyone else.

How well do we treat our loved ones? Why are we so critical of each other? Why do we seem to lack patience and empathy? I believe it is because we are either living in our past, stuck in our past experiences and being trapped by our memories, or we are too worried about the future and what it holds in store for us. I believe that there was no other place for me to go on the day of my father's death. I was done with the past. I was not going to have him in my future, because he was at that very moment leaving the Earth. The only moment I had was there as he left his body and he left his Egoic Mind. All that was left was Pure Soul. His Soul chose to be my father, and my Soul chose to be his daughter. That's going to be a very tough pill to swallow, for some of you who hang on to your Victim Mentality. That's ok. It won't stop me from saying what I know to be true. I AM Authentic. I AM.

Yes, it's true you were "victimized." If you continue to label yourself a victim – you will continue to attract being victimized again in some way, shape or form. You do not do this consciously, of course not. There are Divine Laws happening all the time. They exist whether you believe they do or not. What is floating around in your subconscious, will attract your victim story, if you do not change your thoughts about yourself. When, and if, in this lifetime, you come to the realization that you are so much more than the story you tell yourself. If you realize that you're actually a Soul having a Human Experience, and it's not the other way around, then you will truly understand my words.

To be Self-Actualized is the greatest knowledge of all. This is what truly gives you Wealth. There is no other intelligence, no degree, no book smarts, no Ivy League School that can teach you the Truth of who and what you Truly are. There is no priest, no clergy, no scientist, no person living on this planet who can give you your True Self. You and you alone must do the work. You and you alone must find Yourself. When you question your reasons for doing the things you do, when you question your Ego thoughts, and you find that inner calm that is your Higher Self, you will Know. Know Thyself and To Thy Self BE TRUE.[16]

What is the Identity you want to hold onto for the rest of your life? Is it going to be pain and sorrow or Peace Within Yourself and Happiness? It doesn't matter what happened to you. People suffer horrific things every single day, all over the world. Some give up and cave, diving deep into

---

[16] "Know thyself - Wikipedia." https://en.wikipedia.org/wiki/Know_thyself. Accessed 22 Jul. 2023.

their past pain, and by doing so they give all the power and all the control of their lives to the abusers of their past. The past takes over, and these people will most likely never know happiness ever again. That is just sad. All it takes is a thought. A repeated thought, over and over and over again until your body and your mind believe it.

Nobody can tell you when it's time for you to make that choice. This is something only you can do, and only when you feel ready to take on that challenge for your own Self.

Tony Robbins and Cloe Madanes, teach the Triad[17]. This is where if you want to make a strategic decision about a negative habit/pattern about yourself, you change your Physiology, your Language and your Meaning. For example, I want to stop focusing on my childhood trauma. Being stuck in my past is holding me captive and I want to live in the Now. What affirmation, what positive thought can I tell myself (Language) as I move my body in a strong, physical state? I can practice Yoga, as I say this statement about myself, I can go for a run, repeating the new affirmation/language about myself, I can dance, lift weights and even go for a brisk walk, and I can focus on the new meaning this action and this new physiology creates for me in my Now! This works! It has been proven over and over again. I have participated in several of Tony's excellent programs, and I can attest to the changes I have personally made within myself. Stanford University did a thorough study on what happens on a scientific level. Focus on what you want to change about yourself, and never on your past. Remember: "Where Focus Goes, Energy Flows" ~Tony Robbins.

---

[17] "How to discover your peak state with emotional triad psychology." https://www.tonyrobbins.com/stories/unleash-the-power/discover-your-peak-state/. Accessed 13 Sep. 2023.

ACKNOWLEDGEMENTS

There are far too many people, some alive, and some have moved on to their next Soul Journeys, who have taught me and guided me with their Hearts, their Minds and their Souls. I could probably write an entire book on who they are and exactly what I learned from them and how dearly I love them all.

First and foremost, I want to express my deepest gratitude to my three sons. There is nothing more precious to me than my family, and the love I have for each of you knows no bounds. You mean everything to me. I could not be more proud of the remarkable men you have become. My love for you is eternal. Jay, Chris and Paul, You I Love, Forever.

I have written this book as a legacy and a teaching tool for my grandchildren. I want them to know Grandma did all that she possibly could to make the world a better, more kind and gentle place for them and all of my future grandchildren and great-grandchildren to live in. With all my Heart and Soul, I will Love You Forever.

To Tom, my devoted husband, I say thank you for putting up with me when I was so focused on my writing and my work that I did not look up at you when you walked in the room. For all the times I asked you to not interrupt me, and you quietly stepped away, thank you for your patience and understanding. I will always Love You, Fireboy.

I will simply say Thank You for all the learning, all the love, all you risked, some of you gave All, including death. The pain, suffering and vulnerability you had to endure, the struggles to find your own selves, and the courage you possessed in order to share your Truth with the world inspire me beyond measure. It is because of your work that this woman lived to see another day, told her Truth, manifested her breakthroughs, transformed herself, and contributed her story and her knowledge to the World:

> Jesus Christ. Mother Mary & Joseph. Moses. His Holiness The Dali Lama. Bishop Desmond Tutu, Mahatma Gandhi. Saint Francis of Asissi, Archangel Michael, Archangel Gabriel. Saint Christopher, Saint Matthew, Saint Paul. Saint Teresa of Avilia, Saint Teresa of Calcutta. Martin Luther King, Jr., Ernest Holmes, Dr. Wayne Dyer, Louise Hay, Eckhart Tolle, Dr. Joe Dispenza, Cloe Madanes, Milton Erickson, Carl Jung, Abraham Maslow, Mark and Magali Peysha, Tony Robbins, Sage Robbins, Dr. Jordan Peterson, Caroline Myss, Edgar Cayce, Deepak Chopra, Ram Dass, Gabor Mata, Dean Graziosi, Dr. Norm Shealy, Shakti Gawain, Catherine Ponder, Oprah Winfey, Paramahansa Yogananda, J. Krishnamurti.

Heartfelt Thanks To:

> The Beatles, Jackson Browne, Led Zeppelin, David Bowie, The Who, Roy Orbison, Tina

Turner, Bob Dylan, The Rolling Stones, Johnny Cash, Fleetwood Mac, Tom Petty & The Heartbreakers, The Eagles, Arrowsmith, Queen, The Beach Boys, Heart, Adele, One Republic, Pink, Coldplay, Christina Perri, Lauren Daigle, Sia and always, U2.

Your lives have given me enormous inspiration, coupled with the courage I needed to tell my Truth. Without you living your Truth, I never would be able to live my own. Some of you I have met and spoken with personally, and some I have read about in books, and/or watched movies about your teachings and I thoroughly rocked-out at your concerts. All of your life stories gave me the wisdom, the strength and the courage to allow myself to be vulnerable and speak my truth, with the intention of adding more Love, Empathy and Compassion to a World that Suffers from the Egoic Mind.

✦ I chose to never die with my music still inside me. ✦

EPILOGUE

In America, today is Father's Day, specifically, June 18th, 2023. As I find myself in reflection, engrossed in the act of writing, I am reminded of the significance of this day. Inevitably, my mind drifts to moments past, and though I am aware of the importance of remaining present, it is through this introspection that I truly comprehend the extent of my personal growth and development. Over the decades of my life, the profound anguish and desolation that once consumed me has gradually dissipated allowing me to regain my equilibrium. Instead of being weighed down by sorrow, I am able to articulate my thoughts without succumbing to emotional turmoil. With an outpouring of Divine Intervention, I have managed to liberate my Father from the shackles of pain and turmoil. Why would I not do this for him? He was once a wounded child too.

This metaphorical liberation has enabled me to find solace and serenity amidst the tumultuous emotions that this day inevitably brings forth. Father's Day, a date etched deeply within the collective consciousness, carries an unimaginable weight for countless individuals. It serves as a poignant reminder of absences, losses, and fractures in the familial tapestry. For those who have experienced the loss of a father figure, this day unveils a unique brand of heartache and difficulty. Memories both fond and bittersweet surge to the forefront of our minds, intertwining with the complex emotions that accompany grief. It is a reminder of what once was, of the unconditional love and guidance that was once bestowed upon us. Yet, as we navigate the realm of remembrance, we are confronted with the painful void that now exists.

Father's Day, often celebrated with joyful abandon by those who still possess the privilege of paternal presence, becomes a triggering event for those grappling with the absence of such a figure. We bear witness to the swirling sea of sentiments that encompass longing, melancholy, and the yearning for connection. It is a day marked by an acute awareness of the void left behind, a vivid juxtaposition between celebration and sorrow. As society unites in collective commemoration of fatherhood, it is crucial to recognize and acknowledge the complexity of emotions that envelope this occasion.

We must extend compassion and empathy towards those for whom this day reignites dormant pain. In doing so, we create an atmosphere that fosters healing and understanding, validating the myriad of experiences that exist beneath the surface. On this Father's Day, as I sit here and reflect, I am compelled to share my journey with others who have navigated similar emotional landscapes. Together, we find solace in the power of resilience and the ability to transcend the heartache that once threatened to consume us. While the painful memories persist, they no longer overshadow the strength and growth; the Resilience that has emerged from the depths of our grief.

Ultimately, Father's Day serves as a poignant reminder of the profound impact that paternal figures can have on our lives. Whether marked by celebration or characterized by sorrow, this day unites us in a shared understanding of the intricate tapestry of human experience. It is through embracing both the joyous and the sorrowful moments that we truly honor the legacy and enduring influence of fathers everywhere.

Good, bad or indifferent; all human beings hold the Light within themselves. Regardless of the tragedies, trauma and upbringing we have received, we are all equals as Souls. We are Perfect. We are Whole. We are Complete. We are Light and We Are Love. We are the Perfect Expression of God – our Creator. If we do not express this in our daily lives, it is because we have forgotten who we are.

Printed in the United States
by Baker & Taylor Publisher Services